Simple insights to improve your relationships **– and your life!**

Why is it that in today's 24/7 connected world of Facebook, email and text messaging, many of us feel even more isolated and disconnected than ever before? The answer is that most of us have never learned – or seem to have forgotten – how to connect on a fundamental level. This book brings us back to basics by getting to the heart of what true connection is all about.

- Whether you're a man or a woman, young or old, straight or gay, in a friendship, a family relationship, single, dating, partnered, married or divorced…

- If you'd like to understand how emotional connection is the long-term glue that binds together your personal relationships…

- If you're more interested in the similarities between people – and their universal need for connection – rather than the differences…

- If something seems to be missing from your personal relationships and you can't quite put your finger on it…

- If you're experiencing conflict with your partner, a friend, or a family member and you're having difficulty resolving it…

- If you feel stuck in old, recurring patterns of relating that no longer work for you…

- If your relationships tend to skate along the surface and you want to go deeper…

- If you'd like your personal relationships to change but you don't know where to start…

Then this is the book for you.

THE i FACTOR™

PAUL N. WEINBERG • DR. SUSAN A. DYER

The I Factor Press
10560 Wilshire Blvd. #2004
Los Angeles, CA 90024
info@theifactor.com

Cover and Interior Design: Efrain Salinas

www.theIfactor.com
www.facebook.com/theIfactor
www.twitter.com/theifactor1

ISBN: 978-0-9837459-0-7. 20120601

To my family and closest friends, to Marion Hardie, and especially to my wife, Shay, for being a wonderful partner in intimacy, for allowing me to see her, and for having eyes to see me.

Paul

To my husband, Steve, to Fred Kahane, to my family, and to everyone who has been a part of my world and accepted me as I am into theirs. You have made my world so much richer as a result.

Sue

Special thanks to Dan Adler, Alan Baker, Brent Burghdorf, Deepak Chopra, Alex Emelianov, Lynn Franklin, Caroline Frazer, Ariel Hazi, Nora Hazi, Michael Hoyt, Mark Kurian, Greg Meisel, Carolyn Rangel and Gregory Toprover.

Intimacy is both the ability and the choice to be close, loving, and vulnerable, and typically requires well-developed emotional awareness to sustain for any length of time.

Wikipedia

This book applies to **all** adult personal relationships, including those between romantic partners, friends, and family members, and to existing relationships as well as those in the early stages of development.

So as used in this book, the term **partner** can mean not only romantic partner or spouse, but also friend, family member, or anyone else with whom you would like to have a closer, more connected relationship.

Finally, while **gender differences** certainly exist to varying degrees in every relationship, this book focuses instead on the similarities between men and women in their underlying needs for intimacy and connection.

Paul's Preface

The I Factor™ was a collaborative writing effort with my ex-wife, Susan Dyer, Psy.D. It represents a distillation of what we've learned over the years about creating and sustaining intimate connection, not only in romantic relationships but also with friends and family members.

An ex-husband and wife might seem like an unlikely duo to write a book on intimacy but it's really not as strange as it might seem. When we first met, we both felt an instant sense of comfort and familiarity, and we realized very quickly that we shared a powerful desire for connection with the people in our lives. And while our relationship has developed and grown and changed form over more than two decades, the one constant has been our enduring friendship, sustained by the depth of connection between us.

Despite the connection, our relationship faced challenges that neither of us was equipped at the time to handle. I grew up in a family where no one knew how to express, receive or acknowledge feelings and every conflict became a fact-oriented debate where the goal was to make yourself right and the other person wrong. As a result, it was impossible to connect with anyone in my family, and I felt sad, isolated and alone because my feelings didn't seem to matter. Needless to say, I became an excellent debater, but my argumentative approach to dealing with conflict tended to alienate those around me, including my ex-wife, and often made it difficult for me to achieve the connection that I sought.

And yet, therapy, self-examination and years of practice have helped me to become softer, less focused on winning every argument, and better able to relate to my own feelings and those of the people around me. In turn, my personal relationships have become more serene, satisfying and connected.

The groundwork for this book was laid nearly fifteen years ago, shortly after Sue and I split up. Although our marriage had ended, we continued to work both individually and together in therapy to learn from our mistakes, to grow from our experience, and to avoid making the same mistakes in subsequent relationships.

I eventually started dating again but found myself struggling to connect with the women I met. One woman finally asked me what I wanted in a relationship. My one-word answer was *intimacy*. She asked what that word meant to me, but I didn't have a clear-cut response at the time. So I began compiling a list of short insights that subsequently became the initial foundation for this book.

Over a decade later, I felt compelled to expand on my initial list and write a book that captured the essence of intimacy. I wanted it to be accessible to both women and men, and to address the connection challenges I had faced not only with the women in my life but also with my friends and family. No such book existed.

Meanwhile, Sue and I had continued our separate journeys over the years and had married other partners. At the same time, we'd maintained a close friendship and had each learned valuable lessons about intimacy since we first met.

So when I embarked on the venture of writing this book, I immediately thought of Sue. Her formal training and experience as a clinical psychologist coupled with my initial insights about intimacy and our combined personal experiences – both together and separately – were a natural fit for the creation of this book.

It is our hope that the combination of our male and female perspectives – with an emphasis on our commonality and what brings us together rather than separates us – has allowed us to create something unique and interesting for everyone.

Paul Weinberg

Sue's Preface

If you had asked me twenty years ago what it meant to be in an intimate relationship, my eyes would have glazed over and I would have been rendered mute. I didn't have a clue.

While I had a general sense of what I wanted – and didn't want – in my personal relationships, intimacy wasn't a consideration.

I had little awareness of what it meant to have an intimate relationship or to truly connect with someone. My romantic relationships were based primarily on physical chemistry. My friendships were based on shared interests and activities. And my family relationships were based on shared experiences, childhood memories and family obligations. The common denominator in all of my relationships was that they were mostly superficial. In hindsight, this isn't surprising, given that the relationship I had with myself wasn't much different.

At the same time, there was a part of me that knew something was missing and yearned for something more...

When I first met Paul, I found in him an openness and vulnerability that existed within me but against which I was well-defended. My earlier years were marked by trauma and loss, and I was poorly equipped to deal with the feelings that surfaced. With virtually no outlet for my feelings, I effectively buried them and subsequently built a protective wall around myself. What emerged was a façade of confidence, competence and control behind which were feelings of sadness, fear and frustration.

At my very core, I didn't feel okay about myself. And I unknowingly carried this narrative with me well into adulthood, reacting to situations and people out of fear of rejection when I had already rejected myself long before.

Shortly before Paul and I separated, I remember telling our therapist, "There's nothing wrong with *me*. If only *he* changed, we wouldn't have a problem." It took the failure of our marriage for me to step back and take a hard look at myself, and to fully grasp how unaware I was and how defended and reactive I had become. I needed to drop my guard, open up, and choose a different path.

What started out as a painful process became an ongoing journey filled with wonder, gratitude, and many "aha" moments. It's a journey that has provided me with a more expansive view of both myself and others, enabled me to set healthy boundaries without building a wall around myself, and led me to deeper and stronger connections. And it has brought me a sense of freedom in knowing that I can consciously choose with integrity and authenticity how to respond rather than simply react to whatever arises in my relationships and my life. The insights contained within this book are the outcome of that process.

Few of us have had any formal training on how to have an intimate relationship, and most of us carry wounds from our past that impact our current relationships. We lack awareness of what we bring into our relationships and how much power we have to both positively and negatively affect them. Despite our best intentions and efforts, we often falter in the relationships that mean the most to us and miss out on countless opportunities for connection and intimacy. But through gradual shifts in awareness, language and behavior, and through practice and reinforcement, we can transform our relationships – with ourselves and others – into more nurturing, rewarding and enriching ones.

It is our combined hope that the words we've written in this book will resonate with you, increase your awareness, broaden your perspective, and facilitate greater connection in all of your adult personal relationships.

Sue Dyer

Introduction

We live in an age of unprecedented 24/7 connection, in which Facebook, email, text messaging and other forms of electronic communication have us instantly connected to anyone and everyone around us.

And yet, despite being more connected than ever, many of us are also experiencing a profound and pervasive sense of isolation and disconnectedness. We skate along the surface of our relationships, having swapped quantity for quality and frequency for depth.

The explanation for this seeming contradiction of isolation and disconnectedness in a massively interconnected world is that most of us have never learned – or seem to have forgotten – how to connect or even what it means to connect on a fundamental level.

Connection in the age of social media is even more challenging when electronic communication – including not only emails and texts but also posts, comments, likes and impromptu online chats – seduce us into believing that we are connecting more deeply than we really are. While these forms of communication certainly broaden our *opportunities* to connect, they can also crowd out the more human, meaningful and multi-dimensional ways of interacting, and even create the illusion of intimacy when in fact we are still emotionally disconnected.

And with online connections offering an unprecedented view into other people's lives – but none of the sustenance of deeper, more meaningful relationships – many of us feel even worse that our lives are empty by comparison and simply don't measure up.

The I Factor gets back to basics on what's been missing from our personal relationships all along. Specifically, this book is about *intimacy*, a fresh take on a very old subject and a new way of looking at a forgotten idea.

Because old-fashioned intimacy is really just the deeper level of *connection* that most of us talk about wanting in our personal relationships, but struggle to find in our modern-day lives.

This uniquely approachable book focuses exclusively on intimacy and our universal need for connection with a collection of concise insights that are well-suited for today's fast-paced lifestyle – a book for the wired world of Twitter, sound bites, and short attention spans.

The I Factor breaks a complex topic into straightforward, two-page "chapters," each of which encapsulates just a single text-message-size insight about intimacy plus an email-size nugget of wisdom about each insight.

Unlike many of the best-selling relationship books over the last twenty years, this book emphasizes the similarities rather than the differences between the sexes. And unlike those books, which consider only sexual relationships between romantic partners, this book addresses all of your adult personal relationships, including those with friends and with family members – and most importantly, the one you have with yourself.

Clear and direct, with a bit of humor and a "back-to-basics" approach, this book will increase your awareness of what intimacy is and isn't, and provide a framework for developing more authentic and meaningful connections so that your close personal relationships can be more loving, harmonious and satisfying.

Many of us have some fear associated with the word *intimacy*. And yet, the vast majority of us do want more connection in our lives even if we are scared, confused, don't know where to start, or can't quite figure out what's missing from our relationships.

So whatever you call it – the I factor... intimacy... connection – this book will enhance and sustain your personal relationships, facilitate your own personal growth, and contribute to your overall sense of connectedness, serenity and well-being.

Let the world know you as you are, not as you think you
should be, because sooner or later, if you are posing,
you will forget the pose, and then where are you?

Fanny Brice

Why **Intimacy**

- Allows you to truly know and connect with other people.

- Energizes and enlivens all of your personal relationships.

- Deepens your understanding of yourself and others.

- Creates a sense of belonging and connection in the world.

- Provides what many of us are missing in our lives.

- Allows for more authentic and loving relationships.

- Balances the "I" with the "you" and the "we."

- Helps shift old, unhealthy beliefs and behaviors.

- Broadens and enriches your world.

- Expands your level of awareness.

- Helps you reconnect with yourself.

- Provides a mirror in which to see yourself more clearly.

- Encourages you to deal with complex feelings.

- Enhances sex in the context of a romantic relationship.

- Can mediate the negative effects of stress.

- Improves your overall sense of well-being.

- Helps keep you grounded in today's uncertain world.

- Feels good and nurtures your soul.

- Positively impacts future generations.

I'm not afraid of ghosts. In fact, I'm not afraid of anything. Except perhaps low quarterly profit projections and personal intimacy.

Daffy Duck

How To Use **This Book**

Unlike a typical self-help book with clear-cut "rules" for what to do and what not to do, this book instead provides key insights to be used as *guidelines*.

The authors deliberately left out personal stories so that you can imagine into each insight and how it applies to your own personal relationships.

After all, every relationship is different. Use your own judgment and make each insight personal to you and your particular circumstances.

To get the most out of this book:

- Keep an open mind about yourself and your relationships.
- Assess the level of intimacy you have in your own life.
- Consider your own challenges around intimacy.
- Explore the book alone or together with a partner.
- Use the book to start a dialogue about your relationship.
- Consult the book as a reference in specific situations.
- Take time to reflect on each insight before moving on.
- Adapt and apply each insight to your own situation.
- Remember that the only one you can change is yourself.

Most importantly, use this book as inspiration for creating deeper and more meaningful intimate connections in your life in whatever ways work best for you.

Intimacy is a four syllable word for, "Here is my heart and soul, please grind them into hamburger." It's both desired, and feared. Difficult to live with, and impossible to live without.

Dr. Meredith Grey *(Ellen Pompeo)*
Grey's Anatomy

Contents

Paul's Preface 6

Sue's Preface 8

Introduction 10

Why Intimacy 13

How to Use This Book 15

The Fundamentals 19

Foundations of Intimacy 39

Intimacy and Feelings 65

Intimacy and Differences 85

Intimacy and You 103

Intimacy and Communication 139

Intimacy and Conflict 181

Challenges of Intimacy 221

Intimacy Over Time 247

Summary 275

Epilogue 277

What Now 278

Emotional Intelligence 281

Feelings 282

Needs 285

The I Pyramid 287

The challenge of intimacy is by no means limited to the subject of men, marriage, or romantic encounters, although some of us may equate "intimacy" with images of blissful heterosexual pairings. A primary commitment to a man reflects only one opportunity for intimacy in a world that is rich with possibilities for connectedness and attachment.

Harriet Goldhor Lerner, Ph.D.
The Dance of Intimacy

The Fundamentals

When love is accompanied with deep intimacy, it raises us to the highest level of human experience. In this exalted space, we can surrender our egos, become vulnerable and know levels of joy and well-being unique among life experiences.

·Leo Buscaglia
Born For Love

Love is not intimacy.

Emotional intimacy and love often go together, but love in a relationship does not guarantee intimacy. Specifically, you can have the caring, attachment, and emotional support of love without the emotional availability, openness and vulnerability of intimacy.

Love is just one part of the larger landscape of connection in personal relationships. And it is intimacy rather than love that brings emotional depth to the connection and permits a deeper knowing of yourself and your partner.

Among men, sex sometimes results in intimacy;
among women, intimacy sometimes results in sex.

Barbara Cartland

Sex is not intimacy.

You can have sex without intimacy and intimacy without sex. And although a sexual relationship may lead to an emotionally intimate one, becoming sexual too early in a new relationship may actually interfere with – or be a way to avoid – the development of emotional intimacy.

This may feel like a cold slap in the face if sex is important to you, or you view it as *the* most important part of a romantic relationship.

But sex without an emotional connection is simply a physical connection. The two can be confused if you haven't learned to differentiate between your physical needs and your emotional needs, or if you've learned to get your needs for connection and closeness met – at least temporarily – through sex.

The connection of emotional intimacy in a romantic relationship not only enhances the physical and sexual connection, it is also more enduring.

My wife and I were happy for twenty years.
Then we met.

Rodney Dangerfield

Intimacy is not a feeling.

Intimacy is an enduring state of being within a relationship whereby you and your partner together create the conditions through which deep personal connection can grow. These conditions include trust, openness, vulnerability, safety, empathy and honesty.

By contrast, feelings – happy, sad, angry, afraid, hopeful, helpless, calm, proud, disappointed – are transient states that exist independently *within* you rather than *between* you and your partner.

And while intimacy is not a feeling, it does support the mutual *expression* of feelings, and provides the foundation for enduring connection in all of your personal relationships.

We are so accustomed to disguising ourselves to others
that in the end we become disguised to ourselves

Francois de La Rochefoucauld

Intimacy is the emotional connection between you and your partner.

Rather than simply an attachment or a physical connection, intimacy is about connecting and being connected on an emotional level to your partner.

It is the sharing of your innermost thoughts and feelings, coupled with all the ways of being together – a glance, a touch, a silent moment, a laugh, or just being present and attentive – that provide the foundation for an emotional connection in a personal relationship.

It is also about the emotional connection you have with yourself, without which you cannot have an emotional connection with someone else.

To be connected to yourself means to be able to locate, identify and accept your feelings without self-judgment, to know what you want and need, to be aware of your limits and boundaries, to trust yourself, and to have clarity around what you are willing to accept and tolerate in your relationships.

Intimacy is seeing and being seen by your partner.

Infatuation, lust and the early romantic stages of love are all phases of a relationship that can blind us to the reality of our partner, during which we may project onto them a fantasy that has little or nothing to do with who they are.

By contrast, intimacy is about seeing each other clearly and completely and with as little distortion as possible. This means having a balanced view of your partner by recognizing their weaknesses as well as their strengths. And it starts by having a balanced view of yourself.

In other words, love may be blind but intimacy has 20/20 vision.

Intimacy involves commitment.

Commitment in an intimate relationship has less to do with exclusivity and more to do with a mutual agreement that neither of you is going to flee or abandon the other when conflicts or differences arise.

Even seemingly innocuous statements – or thoughts – can suggest that you already have one foot out the door, aren't fully invested in the relationship, or are not willing to work through conflict.

Uncommitted:

- What do you want me to do about it?
- Why are we together if you feel this way?
- I don't need this.
- I give up.

Committed:

- We can work through this.
- It's okay that we don't agree.
- Let's keep working on it.
- We're in this together.

THE I FACTOR

You cannot have intimacy with everyone.

Being emotionally honest and available invites your partner to do the same, but simply spilling your guts and indiscriminately revealing everything to everyone will not create intimacy.

Intimacy involves a certain amount of exclusivity, and you are more likely to create it if you are discerning about to whom, how, when, and in what context you choose to reveal yourself.

In fact, not everyone in all places or circumstances will want to have an intimate connection with you, nor will it always be appropriate for you to attempt to establish one.

As you venture forward into any relationship, consider the context, pay close attention to the other person's willingness to connect with you, tune into your feelings, and be aware that you may be chasing after someone or something that doesn't really exist.

It is when we stay in a relationship over time – whether by necessity or choice – that our capacity for intimacy is truly put to the test. It is only in long-term relationships that we are called upon to navigate that delicate balance between separateness and connectedness and that we confront the challenge of sustaining both – without losing either when the going gets rough.

Harriet Goldhor Lerner, Ph.D.
The Dance of Intimacy

Intimacy takes time to develop.

Intimacy does not happen immediately. It develops and builds slowly over time through progressive disclosure and a self-reinforcing cycle of trust, safety, and willingness to reveal deeper and deeper layers of yourself.

Genuine intimacy:

- Requires time, effort and patience.
- Starts with small disclosures.
- Considers your partner's willingness to share.
- Pays attention to verbal and nonverbal cues.
- Trust is earned.

False sense of intimacy:

- Assumes you've found your soul mate.
- Reveals everything early on.
- Lacks awareness of your partner.
- Overrides your instincts and intuition.
- Trust is assumed.

My friends tell me I have an intimacy problem.
But they don't really know me.

Garry Shandling

Without intimacy, a relationship – and the world – can be a very lonely place.

A relationship may provide physical companionship and comfort, but you can still feel very lonely even in the presence of your partner without the emotional connection provided by intimacy.

By contrast, intimacy provides you with a sense of belonging, acceptance and connection that helps you feel less alone in the world even when you are physically alone.

Finally, don't confuse being alone with feeling lonely. If you cannot tolerate being alone, you will always be in search of someone else to fill the hole, which only you can do for yourself.

One of the characteristics of relationships that flower
is a relatively high degree of mutual self-disclosure – a
willingness to let our partner enter into the interior of our
private world and a genuine interest in the private world of
that partner.

Nathaniel Branden

Foundations of Intimacy

"You realize, Louise, that in order for our symbiotic relationship to succeed there has to be at least some degree of trust."

Intimacy is built on a foundation of trust.

To be in an intimate relationship, you must be willing to trust your partner, entrust yourself to your partner, and be trustworthy.

First and foremost, though, you must be able to trust yourself. This means that you are clear about your values, boundaries and individual needs, and able to express and act in a way that's consistent with them regardless of external influences.

Trust within a relationship is earned and takes time to establish, and expectations of trust cannot go faster than either partner's level of comfort.

To trust immediately and indiscriminately without any thought will likely lead to betrayal. At the same time, to be unwilling to trust out of fear or past hurt will preclude you from connecting even with those who may be trustworthy.

It is only through trial and error and testing the waters a little bit at a time that you will be able to establish a foundation of trust on which to build an intimate relationship.

What does open us is sharing our vulnerabilities. Sometimes we see a couple who has done this difficult work over a lifetime. In the process, they have grown old together. We can sense the enormous comfort, the shared quality of ease between these people. It is beautiful, and very rare. Without this quality of openness and vulnerability, partners don't really know each other; they are one image living with another image.

Charlotte Joko Beck

Intimacy and vulnerability are intertwined.

Being vulnerable is a prerequisite to having and sustaining an intimate relationship, and is as important as showing your strength, confidence and competence.

While letting your guard down can seem risky or scary, your vulnerability – and letting your partner know that you are vulnerable – makes you more authentic and approachable, sends the message that you trust your partner, and encourages your partner to be vulnerable as well.

Practicing vulnerability in your closest relationships is the key to intimacy.

Intimacy and vulnerability:

- Emotional risks are necessary.
- Defenses are lowered.
- Weaknesses are acknowledged.
- Feelings are expressed.
- Heart-centered.

Ego and defensiveness:

- Emotional risks are avoided.
- Afraid of the unknown.
- Vulnerability is mistaken for weakness.
- Feelings are concealed.
- Head-centered.

If we want to be loved, we must disclose ourselves. If we want to love someone, he must permit us to know him. This would seem to be obvious. Yet most of us spend a great part of our lives thinking up ways to avoid becoming known.

Indeed, much of human life is best described as impersonation. We are role players, every one of us. We say that we feel things we do not feel. We say things we did not do. We say that we believe things we do not believe. We pretend that we are loving when we are full of hostility. We pretend that we are calm and indifferent when we are actually trembling with anxiety and fear.

Of course we cannot tell even the people we know and love everything we think or feel. But our mistakes are nearly always in the other direction. Even in families – good families – people wear masks a great deal of the time.

Sidney Jourard
The Transparent Self

Intimacy is about completely revealing yourself.

In an intimate relationship, you must be willing to take off your mask and be seen for who you are rather than who you think you should be or who you want your partner to think you are.

As much as you want to be seen in the best possible light, you cannot be fully known by your partner unless you present a complete rather than one-sided view of yourself.

This means revealing rather than hiding your weaknesses, shortcomings, sadness, fears, hurts, disappointments, anger and insecurities. They are as much a part of who you are as your strengths, competence, joys, triumphs and self-confidence.

Intimacy in your relationship – and authenticity – begins with you.

Intimacy is feeling safe to reveal yourself.

In order to reveal yourself and be vulnerable in an intimate relationship, it is important that you feel safe within yourself. It also helps to feel safe with your partner.

This means accepting who you are without judgment, and trusting that your partner will not judge you for what you reveal, react negatively, or throw it back in your face.

This does not mean that you and your partner won't have judgments – everyone does – but simply that you become aware of what they are, and are willing to acknowledge and challenge them when they arise.

Until you examine your judgments and what lies beneath them – fear or some disowned part of yourself – you will have difficulty feeling safe within yourself and being vulnerable in your relationships.

DON JUAN DEMARCO

EXT. SITTING ON FRONT LAWN - DAY

                DR. JACK MICKLER (Marlon Brando)
        I need to find out who you are.

                MARILYN MICKLER (Faye Dunaway)
        Jack, you know who I am. Who's brought you
        coffee for the last thirty-two years?

                DR. JACK MICKLER
        Listen, I know a lot about dirty coffee
        cups and I know a lot of facts but I need
        to know all about you.

                MARILYN MICKLER
        What do you want to know?

                DR. JACK MICKLER
        I want to know what your hopes and your
        dreams are. It got lost along the way
        when I was thinking about myself…

        What's so funny?

                MARILYN MICKLER
                (tears)
        I thought you'd never ask.

Intimacy is a two-way street.

Even a one-sided relationship can feel like an intimate connection. For example, your partner may be receptive to your openness while revealing nothing of themselves. Or your partner might turn to you for emotional support during a difficult time while showing no interest in you.

But intimacy is bidirectional. In other words, you and your partner must both be willing to participate, and intimate disclosures must occur in both directions. If only one of you is disclosing, the other one may be a good listener and even a confidante, but you do not necessarily have an intimate relationship.

Be aware and pay attention not only to your partner but also to yourself. If you are typically the listener in your relationship, you might be hiding behind this role so try sharing more of yourself. And if you are typically the one who shares, you might simply be venting so try listening more and showing more interest in your partner.

Ultimately, intimacy is a trial-and-error process that will only reveal itself over time, because what starts out as one-sided may eventually develop into a more balanced two-sided relationship in which each of you is both open and receptive to the other.

Intimacy is not secretive.

Intimacy involves the mutual disclosure – within the safety of the relationship – of thoughts and feelings that you typically keep hidden from everyone else. This includes those parts of yourself that you judge to be unacceptable or unworthy, or behaviors that evoke feelings of guilt or shame.

Secrets are both s e p a r a t i n g

and isolating.

While you may fear that your partner will betray your confidence, that you or your partner may be hurt by what you disclose, or that your partner may judge, reject or abandon you, intimacy cannot exist without taking this risk.

"Jack and I have learned to accept each other's idiosyncrasies, like my passion for cashew brittle, and his going out every night and not coming home until dawn."

Acceptance is key to an intimate relationship.

Intimacy requires that you be accepting of yourself as well as your partner. At the most fundamental level, this means accepting weaknesses as well as strengths.

More significantly, it means accepting rather than judging or rejecting whatever you or your partner is feeling and experiencing at any given moment.

It does not mean accepting behavior that is hurtful or has a negative impact on you.

Rejecting of yourself:

- I shouldn't feel this way.
- What's wrong with me?

Rejecting of your partner:

- You're overreacting.
- You're too sensitive.

Accepting of yourself:

- My feelings are valid.
- I'm feeling this way for a reason.

Accepting of your partner:

- I see where you're coming from.
- I can appreciate your perspective.

The entire sum of existence is the magic of being needed by just one other person.

Vi Putnam

.

Having needs in an intimate relationship is not the same as being needy.

If you confuse *having needs* with *being needy*, you may be afraid to express your own needs in an intimate relationship, and you may judge or reject your partner for theirs.

Needs must be explicitly expressed, whether for affection, attention or emotional support, or simply to be heard.

Neither you nor your partner is a mind reader so don't assume that you know what the other needs. And needs change in different circumstances and over time, so check in with each other periodically.

Having the courage to express your needs creates an opportunity for you to get your needs met.

Not judging or rejecting your partner for being needy is an opportunity for you to meet their needs.

Expressing your needs:

- Keep it simple.
- Be specific and explicit.
- Start with "I" rather than "you."
- Make a request, not a demand.
- Use positive rather than negative language.

There is no greater challenge than to have someone
relying upon you; no greater satisfaction than to vindicate
his expectation.

Kingman Brewster, Jr.

Intimacy involves mutual reliance.

In an intimate relationship, you and your partner must each be willing and able to rely upon the other, which takes trust, vulnerability, and a willingness to surrender control.

At the same time, each of you must be willing and able to be reliable, which takes maturity, accountability and responsibility.

An essential element of reliance is knowing each other's expectations, which can only occur if they are explicitly stated and agreed upon.

Being reliable:

- Mean what you say.
- Clarify expectations.
- Avoid making promises you can't keep.
- Follow through on commitments.
- Communicate when plans change.

"You make me feel insignificant. You treat me like a child. You belittle me. You don't like my friends, you get angry with me when I see them, you don't want me to succeed, you undermine me, nothing I say is correct, I can't even choose a movie or order DINNER, you think the things I'm interested in are ridiculous, everything is rational and calculated to you, you're not supportive of my work, you don't want to take me seriously, you want to own me and control everything, but people aren't like -- you can't run their lives or derive your security from possessing them. You can't expect me to spend my life trying to be what you think I should be."

BUT I LOVE YOU.

machlis

Intimacy involves mutual respect.

An intimate relationship is one in which you and your partner respect, accept and support each other. It is not abusive, oppressive, controlling or coercive. Nor is it one where you must lose, betray or sacrifice yourself or your hopes and dreams to be in the relationship.

This means approaching each other as equal participants in the relationship even if you are not able to contribute equally, even if there is a power differential between you, and even if one of you is in a position to pull the rug out from under the other.

Be courteous to all, but intimate with few, and let those few be well tried before you give them your confidence.

George Washington

Intimacy involves confidentiality.

Treating disclosures confidentially and not repeating or sharing them with a third party without your partner's consent respects the sanctity of your relationship and is fundamental to intimacy.

This means that it's up to each of you to state a clear position with regard to how you maintain boundaries, as well as how you cope with the competing demands and conflicts among other members of a group with whom you have intimate relationships.

If you do not know which disclosures are confidential, then ask. If you are not certain that your partner understands that what you have disclosed needs to be treated confidentially, say so explicitly.

Humor is imperative in an intimate relationship.

Sharing a laugh, playing, being silly together, and even telling jokes are all forms of intimacy.

Humor – as long as it's not at your partner's expense – can also break the tension or silence during times of stress or conflict.

Maintaining a sense of humor and being able to laugh at yourself and your circumstances can shift an otherwise difficult or unbearable interaction to a tolerable and even enjoyable one.

Be who you are and say what you feel,
because those who mind don't matter,
and those who matter don't mind.

Dr. Seuss

Intimacy and Feelings

Though we may think we know each other well, when we neglect feelings in a relationship, we neglect the deepest and most intimate part of ourselves… Sharing feelings leads us to great closeness because feelings are very personal, the most intimate part of us. The sharing of a deep feeling is the greatest gift a human being can give to another.

Father Chuck Gallagher

Intimacy is heart-centered not head-centered.

Intimacy is about approaching your partner and the relationship from your heart rather than your head. This means empathizing with your partner's experience rather than intellectualizing, analyzing, dismissing, judging or arguing with it.

While you can know each other through your thoughts and actions, your very essence and innermost reality is captured through your feelings.

It is through feelings that you can truly know, understand and love each other for who you are.

Feelings rather than thoughts are the lifeblood of intimacy.

Intimacy may include affection as well as shared beliefs, values and attitudes, but the sharing of feelings is the basis of the emotional connection between you and your partner.

Revealing your feelings is disarming, allows you to become more fully known and understood, enables clearer and more effective communication, and can bring you and your partner closer together even when the feelings themselves are unpleasant.

And the emotional bond created by the exchange of feelings can carry you through the rough times and enable you to remain connected even in the midst of conflict.

Sharing feelings is the hallmark of intimacy.

Intimacy involves being aware of your own feelings, and being willing and able to openly and honestly express them to your partner. At the same time, it is about being receptive, sensitive and responsive to your partner's feelings.

Expressing your feelings means clearly communicating them rather than venting them in a way that blames or attacks your partner.

Being receptive to your partner's feelings means accepting them as valid without feeling blamed or responsible for them.

Your task is not to seek for love, but merely to seek and find all the barriers within yourself that you have built against it.

Rumi

Revealing your feelings is not a weakness; it is the path to intimacy.

In the context of an intimate relationship, it is a strength to be able to let down your guard and reveal your feelings.

Even if it causes you or your partner some temporary discomfort, the very process of revealing your feelings indicates that you are willing to risk being vulnerable and fully known, and that the relationship is important to you.

By contrast, denying your feelings or keeping them bottled up inside can create distance, reduce safety, undermine trust, and lead to resentment over time.

And at the most fundamental level, denying your feelings denies an integral part of who you are – the very essence of what makes you human.

"I can't wait 'til we're so close we don't have to talk."

Intimacy is about saying what you feel, not what you think.

Saying what you feel in an intimate relationship may seem obvious, but you may mistakenly label as feelings what are actually your thoughts, opinions, perceptions, assumptions or judgments.

By contrast, *actual* feeling statements express your true underlying feelings along with the deepest and most vulnerable parts of who you are.

"Non-feeling" feeling statements:

- I feel that...
- I feel you are...
- I have a feeling that...
- It feels as if you...
- I feel it's...

Feeling statements:

- I feel sad...
- I feel angry...
- I feel anxious...
- I feel lonely...
- I feel frustrated...
- I feel scared...
- I feel ashamed...

You are not responsible for your partner's feelings in an intimate relationship.

Intimacy gives you the power to affect your partner both positively and negatively. Along with that comes the responsibility to be present, sensitive and responsive to your partner's feelings and needs.

At the same time, you are *not* responsible for your partner's feelings. You *are* responsible for your choices, actions, behavior, and how you respond to your partner.

Be aware that when your partner shares their feelings, they are not looking for you to fix it, offer advice, take their feelings on, agree with them, or convince them that they are wrong. Rather, they are most likely looking for acknowledgement, understanding and support as they voice and work through their feelings on their own.

I can be with my feelings.

I just don't want to be with your feelings.

Bruce Eric Kaplan

Your partner is not responsible for your feelings in an intimate relationship.

Your feelings are the combined result of your thoughts, perceptions and life experiences. They belong to you and are your sole responsibility.

So while your partner's actions and behaviors may negatively affect you and trigger certain feelings within you, your partner cannot *make* you feel a certain way.

While it may be up to your partner to listen, empathize, and accept responsibility for their actions, it is up to you to own, reflect upon, and express your feelings in a way that doesn't victimize you or blame your partner.

Owning your feelings is empowering. Relinquishing responsibility for them is victimizing.

Owning:	Relinquishing:
▪ I'm sad…	▪ I feel rejected…
▪ I'm scared…	▪ I feel abandoned…
▪ I'm frustrated…	▪ I feel unheard…
▪ I'm angry…	▪ I feel betrayed…
▪ I'm anxious…	▪ I feel abused…
▪ I'm lonely…	▪ I feel manipulated…

True, we can have too much challenge, too much uncertainty. However, if we look closely, we'll find that that only happens when we've become too attached to outcomes. In the moment of that realization, our challenge becomes "How well can we learn to let go and stay engaged?" That's a real trick. The real trick.

Tom Atlee
Crisis Fatigue

Intimacy is sometimes about simply sitting with your feelings.

Sometimes the hardest thing to do in an intimate relationship is simply be with your feelings, or let your partner be with theirs.

This means not reacting impulsively without thought or reflection, and instead giving yourself the time and space to locate, identify and feel your feelings.

It also means letting go of any preconceived notions about how you or your partner "should" feel as well as the emphasis on outcome, closure and immediate resolution.

The more you are able to do this, the more you will be able to respond from a heart-centered and balanced perspective rather than a reactive or egocentric one.

"Are you open, emotionally?"

You can't share your feelings if you aren't first able to locate them.

Your
  feelings
    are
      in
        there.
       If
          you
            have
              difficulty
                identifying
              or
                  connecting
                with
                  them,
                  find
                    someone
                    who
                      can
                    help
                      you.

Share our similarities, celebrate our differences.

M. Scott Peck
The Road Less Traveled

Intimacy and Differences

The beginning of love is to let those we love be perfectly themselves, and not to twist them to fit our own image. Otherwise we love only the reflection of ourselves we find in them.

Thomas Merton

Intimacy allows for personal differences.

In the early stages of a relationship, there is a focus on similarities and common interests, but as the relationship develops further, differences become more apparent.

Even though these differences may lead to misunderstandings and disagreements, intimacy is about acknowledging, respecting, accepting, and ultimately embracing them.

As long as they don't require you to compromise a core value, use your differences as an opportunity to grow and learn more about yourself and your partner rather than as a way to make each other wrong.

Accepting and respecting differences minimizes conflict, frees each of you to be yourself in the relationship, and strengthens the connection between you.

"You haven't said anything for ten years. Is everything O.K.?"

Intimacy allows for differences in timing.

Just as everyone has a different need for closeness within an intimate relationship, everyone has a different speed at which they process their experiences and feelings and are ready to communicate them.

Even if you are ready to engage in a dialogue, your partner may need more time to reflect upon and process the situation and their own feelings about it. This takes patience and a willingness to sit with the unknown, and includes checking in with your partner about when it's time to reengage.

ANNIE HALL

ALVY AND ANNIE ARE SEEING THEIR THERAPISTS
AT THE SAME TIME ON A SPLIT SCREEN

ALVY SINGER'S THERAPIST
How often do you sleep together?

ANNIE HALL'S THERAPIST
Do you have sex often?

ALVY SINGER (Woody Allen)
(lamenting)
Hardly ever. Maybe three times a week.

ANNIE HALL (Diane Keaton)
(annoyed)
Constantly. I'd say three times a week.

Intimacy allows for differences in priorities.

Intimacy doesn't mean that you and your partner will always have the same values, concerns and priorities.

When differences arise, distinguish between those that do and do not directly affect you, work together to reach an understanding on those that do, and most importantly, learn to let go of those that do not.

In other words, decide what really matters.

Given the background of my experience, I make sense and order out of my world in one way. Given the background of your experience, you make sense and order out of your world in another way. My way is valid for me; your way appears to be valid for you. That is one of the differences between us in a relationship in which each of us cherishes the other and validates the other's way of being in the world.

Mendel H. Lieberman
Resolving Conflict: Everybody Wins

Intimacy allows for differences in strengths.

Each of you has different strengths and weaknesses. When these differences create conflict, recognize that intimacy is about working through them together with a focus on a collaborative solution that leaves each of you better off than you would have been separately.

Even if you aren't able to meet halfway, you can still bridge the differences and remain connected, each according to your own particular abilities.

There is no such thing as "too sensitive" in an intimate relationship.

Different people have different sensitivities. Even what you view as humor or a minor issue might be hurtful or problematic to your partner.

Whether you are able to hear and respect these differences rather than dismiss or judge them will determine if the level of intimacy in your relationship will continue to grow – or not.

In fact, sensitivity is a skill that can detect issues before they get out of hand. If you or your partner is sensitive about something, you may be picking up on a potential problem in your relationship or becoming aware of something that needs to change.

Sensitivity in certain areas can also be seen as "hot spots" that with curiosity and encouragement can allow you to identify past hurts or traumas. Once brought out into the open, these old wounds can then be explored and healed.

You are the person who has to decide.
Whether you'll do it or toss it aside.

You are the person who makes up your mind.
Whether you'll lead or will linger behind.

Whether you'll try for the goal that's afar.
Or just be contented to stay where you are.

Edgar A. Guest

Different people have different capacities for intimacy.

Your capacity for intimacy is shaped by your family history, past experience, and level of psychological development. It depends largely upon your degree of awareness and whether you are able to access, share and receive feelings. So what comes naturally to you or to your partner may be a struggle – or even seem impossible – for the other.

At the same time, you and your partner are constantly redefining yourselves and co-creating your relationship through each and every interaction you have with each other.

So while your capacities for intimacy may differ, you can still affect the level of intimacy in the relationship by working at it, working on yourself, and providing a healthy model for it.

Providing a healthy model for intimacy:

- You can't demand it; you can only be it.
- Be open and be receptive to openness.
- Be vulnerable and remain vulnerable.
- Focus on change within yourself.
- Be how you want to be in the relationship.
- Be more of what you expect your partner to be.
- Avoid judging or blaming your partner.
- Be patient.

Marcie made the foolish mistake of telling
Herb that she needed her space.

Intimacy is a balance between connectedness and separateness.

An intimate relationship involves connecting with your partner and letting your partner connect with you.

At the same time, intimacy involves establishing, maintaining and respecting personal boundaries.

The challenge is to accept differences between your respective needs for autonomy and attachment without either of you pushing away or chasing after the other.

Intimacy is not for everyone.

Not everyone wants intimacy in their relationships, nor is everyone capable of it.

You cannot have an intimate relationship with someone who is cut off from their feelings, actively addicted, or unwilling to acknowledge their fears and vulnerabilities.

For some, intimacy is simply too risky or threatening, and no matter how much effort you put into the relationship, it will not progress or deepen.

If your partner tells you – through their words or behavior – that they have a problem with intimacy, believe it. Despite your best efforts to connect, your partner may not yet be willing or able to have an intimate relationship with you.

At the end of the day, the best you can do is be clear about your own needs and feelings, be as authentic and transparent as you can be, and behave in a way that is consistent with your values and the level of intimacy you want in the relationship – even if that means leaving the relationship and moving on.

For a relationship to flourish, there must be intimacy. It takes an enormous amount of courage to say, "This is me. I'm not proud of it – in fact, I'm a little embarrassed by it – but this is who I am."

Bill Hybels

Intimacy and You

You must first know and be intimate with yourself to be intimate with someone else.

Intimacy starts by having an intimate relationship with yourself. This means being aware of your feelings, and being willing to actually feel and reflect upon them rather than deny, judge, dismiss or blindly vent them.

It also includes an awareness of your needs, self-judgments and weaknesses – even those you may not want to admit to yourself – and compassionately embracing all aspects of who you are.

Unless you are in touch with the authentic you – *underneath* your persona or ego – it will be difficult, if not impossible, for your partner to fully know you, understand you, or feel connected with you.

Being authentic:

- Guard down; no façade.
- Honest, genuine and forthcoming.
- Speaking from your deepest truth.
- Thoughts and feelings congruent with actions.
- Behavior consistent with values and principles.

The voyage of discovery lies not in finding new landscapes, but in having new eyes.

Marcel Proust

Intimacy offers a mirror in which to see yourself more completely.

Your partner is in a unique position to reflect back to you – either directly or indirectly – sides of yourself that you might otherwise be unable to see on your own. So as much as you may think you already know yourself, there will always be blind spots that are outside of your own view.

You can choose to defend, deny or reject what is being reflected back to you – and be confronted with it again in another relationship – or you can trust that there may be some truth to it and use it as an opportunity for self-discovery and personal growth.

"I'm sorry, dear, I must have lost consciousness.
What were you saying?"

Intimacy requires your presence.

Being present in an intimate relationship does not mean simply your physical presence, since you can be present physically but miles away emotionally.

Presence is being aware of and tuned into your partner's feelings as well as your own – without judgment, analysis or interpretation – in the *present* and without ruminating over the past or worrying about the future.

Presence also includes the emotional depth to process complex and often conflicting feelings in a balanced, thoughtful and nonreactive way.

It is through your presence that you have the power to not only maintain or shift your own emotional state but also affect that of your partner.

When we honestly ask ourselves which person in our lives mean the most to us, we often find that it is those who, instead of giving advice, solutions, or cures, have chosen rather to share our pain and touch our wounds with a warm and tender hand. The friend who can be silent with us in a moment of despair or confusion, who can stay with us in an hour of grief and bereavement, who can tolerate not knowing, not curing, not healing and face with us the reality of our powerlessness, that is a friend who cares.

Henri J.M. Nouwen
The Road to Daybreak: A Spiritual Journey

You must have empathy in order to have intimacy.

More than just showing concern for your partner's feelings – whether or not they are explicitly expressed – intimacy requires empathy, which is the ability to imagine into your partner's experience and get a deep sense of what it feels like to be in their shoes.

Even if you wouldn't feel the same as your partner under similar circumstances, you can still empathize by relating to their feelings. You've most likely experienced the same feelings at some point in your life, even if it was about something else.

Empathy not only enables your partner to feel supported and understood, it also deepens the level of connection between you.

Empathic responding:

- Consider your partner's frame of reference.
- Tune into your partner's feelings.
- Suspend judgment and reactivity.
- Help clarify underlying feelings and concerns.
- Focus on being with, not changing feelings.
- Avoid "taking on" your partner's feelings.
- Resist the urge to give opinions and advice.
- Soften your tone.

Now the human species is the only species on the planet, of course, that has a relationship with itself. Where you have a relationship with yourself – that's normal. But the cat doesn't have a relationship with itself. Or the bird doesn't have a relationship with itself. Or the tree doesn't. So, birds, cats, trees, monkeys, flowers none of them have a problem with self-esteem. And even the most ugly looking cat wouldn't have a problem with self-esteem. It hasn't created a secondary, an "image self" – mind created. And once that's created it walks with you, next to you, or behind you, or wherever it is. You always walk with a mental image of "me" and you have a relationship with that. And, often you don't like what you see.

Eckhart Tolle
The Power of Now

Intimacy is egoless.

Your ego may serve you well in the workplace or other arenas in which you are expected to perform or compete. It can also provide you with psychological defenses in situations that you perceive as threatening to your sense of self. Unfortunately, your ego can also become a liability in your intimate relationships if you are not aware of it.

It may be helpful to distinguish between the *healthy* ego, the part of us that can observe and reflect upon ourselves, others and situations, and helps us to respond thoughtfully and responsibly, and the *neurotic* ego, the part of us that reacts blindly and is driven by fear, desire, or a need to control. It's the latter that can create an obstacle to intimacy.

So when you find yourself overly focusing on your partner, emphasizing the facts and trying to be right, making judgments, becoming defensive or aggressive, or puffing yourself up and diminishing your partner, it's generally a sign that your ego has taken over and is coming between you.

The challenge is not only to become aware of when your ego is being activated but also to identify and share with your partner the underlying feelings, such as fear, shame, helplessness, inadequacy or disappointment. Only then can the surface limitations of ego give way to the depth of intimacy.

Fill each other's cup
but drink not from one cup.

Give one another of your bread
but eat not from the same loaf.

Sing and dance together and be joyous,
but let each one of you be alone,

Even as the strings of a lute are alone
though they quiver with the same music.

And stand together, yet not too near together;
For the pillars of the temple stand apart,

And the oak tree and the cypress
grow not in each other's shadow

Khalil Gibran
The Prophet

Intimacy is about balancing the "I" with the "you" and the "we."

An intimate relationship includes three distinct entities – you, your partner and the relationship itself.

Each of you must maintain your own separate identity – interests, needs, boundaries, values, friends – while creating and maintaining a mutual identity within the relationship.

Remember that you bring your own issues, needs, and expectations into the relationship, and it is not your partner's obligation to help you resolve, fulfill or meet them all of the time.

When you have *conflicting* needs, or individual needs that conflict with the needs of the relationship, the real challenge is to establish a balance that works for both of you and an explicit protocol for negotiating whose needs get met and when.

You must be able to set boundaries in an intimate relationship.

Intimacy requires that you clearly define the personal boundaries that maintain your individual integrity and sense of self with respect to your partner.

At the same time, you and your partner must agree upon the relationship boundaries that define and maintain the sanctity of the relationship with respect to the rest of the world.

Defining boundaries:

- Know what they are.
- Consider why they are important to you.
- Have an open conversation with your partner.
- Clearly state what is and is not acceptable.
- Never compromise your values or integrity.

Simple solution for a happy relationship

Intimacy respects your individual needs.

In an intimate relationship, your individual needs and values need to be honored and respected as much as those of the relationship.

As do those of your partner.

If either of you surrenders or subverts them in order to avoid conflict or to please or manipulate the other, one of you will end up feeling resentful or losing yourself in the relationship.

Modified golden rule for an intimate relationship: treat your partner not as *you* would like to be treated but rather as you know *they* would like to be treated. And if you don't know, ask!

We look for this security by fortifying and enclosing ourselves in innumerable ways. We want the protection of being "exclusive" and "special," seeking to belong to the safest church, the best nation, the highest class, the right set, and the "nice" people. These defenses lead to divisions between us, and so to more insecurity demanding more defenses.

Alan W. Watts
The Wisdom of Insecurity

Intimacy requires that you be conscious of your own anxieties.

Anxiety arises out of your ego's need to protect itself. It can interfere with your ability to be open and receptive to your own feelings as well as those of your partner. It can also cause you to become reactive or to shut down altogether.

If you are feeling anxious, sometimes simply acknowledging it to your partner, slowing down, and looking at what may be fueling it can help reduce the anxiety and maintain the connection between you.

Exploring the possible source of the anxiety, digging deeper into the underlying feelings or judgments associated with it, and focusing on the present will enable you to reconnect with yourself.

Possible sources of anxiety:

- Old beliefs.
- Past experiences.
- Fear of failure or loss.
- Unresolved family issues.
- Conflicting thoughts or feelings.
- Fear of rejection or abandonment.
- Feelings of guilt or shame.
- Fear of losing control.
- Secrets.

Going to deeper levels of intimacy can feel like falling into an abyss.

An intimate relationship can be uncomfortable and even distressing when it stirs up issues and feelings that you typically keep hidden from others and even from yourself.

In fact, the partner with whom you choose to have an intimate relationship will inevitably become the one who helps bring them to the surface.

These times provide a unique opportunity for you to get to know yourself more fully by digging deeper and working through the underlying issues.

Keep in mind that your partner is likely just the *catalyst* not the *cause* of your discomfort.

Working through underlying issues:

- Be fearless.
- Maintain an internal focus.
- Avoid blaming your partner.
- Use your feelings as a guide.
- Be curious about what comes up.
- Keep pushing when you hit an edge.
- Be open to discovering something new.

Your partner is not responsible for fulfilling all of your needs in an intimate relationship.

It is your responsibility to know your own needs and to express them to your partner.

It is your partner's choice – not their responsibility – whether or not to fulfill them.

If a certain need can't be met by your partner, look at the broader context of the relationship and consider whether you can adjust your expectations, reach a compromise, or find alternatives for getting it met that don't violate your own integrity or that of the relationship.

The bottom line is that it is unlikely that one person can meet all of your needs all of the time, including your needs for connection and intimacy.

And ultimately, it is up to you to decide if enough of your needs are being met enough of the time to warrant staying in the relationship.

We don't see things as they are.
We see things as we are.

Anais Nin

Intimacy is internally rather than externally focused.

Intimacy is about looking inward and focusing on your own internal experience rather than projecting onto your partner.

When you find yourself labeling or judging your partner or anyone in general, be aware that you are likely projecting some disowned or unacceptable part of yourself – feelings, thoughts or characteristics – onto the other.

Labels and judgments create distance and separation within your relationship, and keep you from fully knowing yourself as well as from truly seeing and knowing your partner.

When you are able to own those parts of yourself that you view in a negative light and embrace all aspects of who you are, including those that are not consistent with your ego's view of itself, you open yourself up to more loving, compassionate and authentic relationships.

Intimacy embraces both the masculine and the feminine.

Despite the obvious differences between the sexes, both men and women have the same universal needs for connection and to be seen, heard, felt, respected, nurtured and loved in an intimate relationship.

More important is an awareness that male and female, which are about gender, are not the same as masculine and feminine, which are complementary qualities that exist in each of us regardless of gender.

While you may have been conditioned to identify with the set of qualities typically associated with your gender, you will be more balanced and whole and will have less conflict within yourself and your relationships when you can embrace and value both sets – and learn to move fluidly between them.

"Masculine" qualities:	**"Feminine" qualities:**
• Logical	• Emotional
• Analytical	• Intuitive
• Rational	• Creative
• Solution-oriented	• Feeling-oriented
• Assertive	• Receptive
• Competitive	• Cooperative
• Independent	• Relational
• Focus on doing	• Focus on being

You have to drop all your defenses, only then is intimacy possible. We are all hiding a thousand and one things, not only from others but from ourselves.

Osho
Intimacy

The irony of intimacy is that you will choose a partner who taps into your old wounds.

An intimate relationship will push you over edges and into vulnerable places that you may have learned to protect out of past hurt or disappointment.

You can choose either to stay in your protected place and remain emotionally stagnant, or trust that the relationship will provide you with an opportunity and a safe environment in which to heal those wounds so that you can grow and move beyond them.

Be aware that as you open your heart to your partner, it's not only what you let in but also what might tumble out that may surprise you.

Reactivity in an intimate relationship is a signal to look inside yourself.

The partner you choose often embodies – and is in the unique position to trigger – those parts of yourself that are less developed, from which you are disconnected, or to which you are not giving a voice.

Your reactivity to your partner – and often what you like least about them – can be a clue that these parts are being triggered. These times provide a valuable opportunity to break reactive patterns and take a fearless look inside yourself.

When you feel the urge to react, slow down, take a breath, think about what you are feeling, and keep in mind that what bothers you is likely to relate back to one of your own issues or some disowned part of yourself.

Put another way, "If you spot it, you've got it."

Intimacy provides an opportunity for personal growth.

Most of us have had imperfect childhoods, and few of us have escaped the experiences of shame, blame, judgment and rejection. As adults, we may then unknowingly recreate with our intimate partner the same emotional dynamics or patterns of relating that we learned within our family of origin.

Paradoxically, it's the very challenges you encounter within your intimate relationships – especially during conflict or when expectations for your partner and the relationship are not met – that enable you to grow.

Growth occurs when you are willing to look within yourself rather than focusing on your partner, and you become aware of how your earlier life experiences – and the feelings associated with them – may be contributing to your current reactions.

Only then can you start to allow the healthy adult parts of yourself to *respond* rather than the wounded child within you to *react*.

Be patient. Growth is not an event; it's a process.

Intimacy is all about you... and not all about you

Intimacy is about you in that it is about revealing yourself to your partner, and it ultimately all comes back to you from the standpoint of personal growth and responsibility.

At the same time, it's not all about you because you cannot begin to lay the groundwork for intimacy unless you are also able to set your ego aside, allow your partner to reveal themselves to you, and be receptive to what is being shared.

The way we communicate with others and with ourselves
ultimately determines the quality of our lives.

Anthony Robbins

Intimacy and Communication

The five levels of communication:

1. **Clichés.** Typical, routine, oft repeated comments, questions and answers given out of habit and with no real forethought or genuine intent. "How are you?" "Fine." "Having a good day?" "Yes."

2. **Facts.** Information/statistics about the weather, the office, friends, the news, personal activities, etc. Requires no in-depth thinking or feeling.

3. **Opinions.** Includes concerns, expectations, and personal goals, dreams, and desires. Due to differences of opinion that naturally arise between two people, especially between men and women, this is typically the level at which we run into the "wall of conflict."

4. **Feelings.** Having gone through the wall of conflict, you both feel safe to share your deepest emotions.

5. **Needs.** The deepest level of communication and intimacy where you feel completely safe to reveal your unique needs with each other. Truly, unless needs are known and met, a couple will remain "strangers."

Gary Smalley
Secrets to Lasting Love

The emotional resonance of intimacy goes beyond the exchange of words.

Intimacy is not simply about common interests, great conversations, or intellectual compatibility. The exchange of information, ideas, thoughts and opinions represents just one level of connection.

Intimacy is about communication that goes beneath the surface. It is the counterpart to love that involves deeper levels of communication, conveyed not only through the sharing of feelings and emotional needs but also through tone, facial expression, body language and touch.

Intimacy exists at the deepest level where each of you is able to not only feel and understand the other but also be felt and understood by the other.

Intimacy is clear and direct.

Intimacy is about authentic and straightforward communication. There are no assumptions or hidden agendas, nor is there any manipulation, sarcasm, game playing, acting out, or passive-aggressive "tit-for-tat" behavior.

This means having clarity within yourself, knowing your intentions, and being honest about how you feel and are affected. It also means expressing yourself assertively rather than passively or aggressively, and communicating in language your partner is most likely to understand.

Finally, recognize the subjective nature of your perceptions and what you bring to the interaction, and also that your partner experiences what you say through their own subjective perspective as well. And even if your partner is unable to receive what you are saying, remember that speaking your truth is important for your own clarity and edification.

"Since we're both being honest, I should tell you I have fleas."

Intimacy is about open and honest communication... but not unnecessary disclosure.

Intimacy is being willing and able to talk about almost anything. This means making time to talk about things that are important to you or your partner, including the relationship itself, and also being direct about what you like – and don't like – about each other or yourself.

This does not mean you must answer every question asked of you, nor share every random thought or feeling that arises within you, some of which are better kept to yourself.

The fine line between honesty and unnecessary disclosure is whether such disclosure is relevant to the relationship, or might be to your partner.

If you are uncertain where to draw the line or need time for reflection, you can still maintain the connection by letting your partner know that you are not yet ready to share what's on your mind. Then make sure to follow up when you are.

Intimacy is about communicating your emotional state in real-time.

Intimacy means being willing and able to openly express your feelings and needs as completely as possible, as they arise, and as you become aware of them in the moment. This is true even if those feelings are ambivalent, confusing, or you are having difficulty coping with them.

This doesn't mean venting them or recklessly acting them out, without any thought or awareness of your environment or how your partner may be affected.

It simply means being willing to bring them out into the open where you can process them in a balanced way rather than hiding them behind a frozen smile or a wall of resentment, hostility or silence.

Intimacy is not about giving advice or fixing a problem.

Despite your best intentions and natural instinct to want to give advice or immediately fix a problem, intimacy first requires your emotional presence – that you listen to, empathize with, reflect back, and validate your partner's feelings and experience – so that your partner feels seen and heard.

Advice giving:

- Why don't you…
- You should…
- The best way to handle this is…
- If it were me, I would…
- You need to…
- Have you tried…

Emotionally present:

- How do you feel about that?
- I can see this is really painful.
- I'm sorry you're going through this.
- What's the worst part of it?
- I'm here to support you.
- What do you need right now?

Our conversations invent us. Through our speech and our silence, we become smaller or larger selves. Through our speech and our silence, we diminish and enhance the other person, and we narrow or expand the possibilities between us. How we use our voice determines the quality of our relationships, who we are in the world, and what the world can and might become. Clearly, a lot is at stake here.

Harriet Goldhor Lerner, Ph.D.
The Dance of Connection

Intimate communication requires an awareness of tone and nonverbal cues.

Your partner will be more receptive to you if you communicate respect and compassion in your tone.

This may seem obvious, but when you are feeling hurt, disappointed or angry, your tone can easily become harsh, blaming, aggressive or matter-of-fact.

And even if you think your tone is fine, be aware of nonverbal cues such as snickering, crossing your arms, pointing your finger, or rolling your eyes.

In other words:

Words + Tone + Nonverbal Cues = Message

Be mindful...

- Watch yourself as you speak.
- Observe your body language.
- Monitor your internal dialogue.
- Attend to shifts in your feelings.
- Notice sensations in your body.
- Be aware of the rate/rhythm of your speech.
- Correct your tone as you notice any changes.

I was sad one day and went for a walk;
I sat in a field.

A rabbit noticed my condition and came near.

It often does not take more than that to help at times –

to just be close to creatures who
are so full of knowing,
so full of love
that they don't –
chat,

they just gaze with
their marvelous understanding.

St. John of the Cross
A Rabbit Noticed My Condition

You cannot multitask intimacy.

You must be fully present and give your partner your undivided attention during an intimate exchange.

You will have more difficulty connecting when either one of you is doing something else, is preoccupied or distracted – either internally or externally – or allows yourself to be interrupted.

If you are unable to be present, let your partner know. Then follow up by making a time that works best for both of you and be sure to follow through.

Internal distractions:

- Physical discomfort.
- Emotional stress.
- Hunger.
- Fatigue.

External distractions:

- Children.
- Deadlines.
- Obligations.
- Electronic devices.

Intimacy includes a willingness to reveal all aspects of who you are.

Even if you've been conditioned to focus on the positive and remain upbeat all the time...

Even if you grew up in an environment where it was unsafe to show who you truly are...

Even if you don't want to burden your partner with your own issues or conflicts...

Even if it causes either you or your partner some discomfort...

The point of intimacy is to allow your partner to see all of you, not just the parts you view as positive, appealing or acceptable.

"Denise, I can read you like a book.
Something's bothering you, isn't it?"

Intimacy requires that you check in – not out – when you feel disconnected.

When you feel disconnected from your partner, your initial reaction may be to withdraw or to override your feelings. While this may seem helpful in the short term, it can widen the gap and make reconnecting more and more difficult over time.

If you sense some distance or separation, consider opening up and checking it out with your partner rather than interpreting it or making assumptions.

Talking about your internal state by sharing what you observe, how you feel, and what you need – without attributing blame – will often help to reestablish the connection.

Communicating your internal state:

- I'm feeling a little distant.
- Something doesn't feel right between us.
- I need a hug.
- I miss you.

Checking on your partner's state:

- Are you okay?
- Is something bothering you?
- I noticed you are more quiet than usual.
- How are you feeling?

People with extraordinary minds talk about ideas.

People with average minds talk about events.

People with simple minds talk about other people.

·Anonymous

Gossiping about other people is not intimacy.

Gossip is an entrenched part of our culture that can serve various social functions and satisfy certain social needs.

Gossip can be used to form superficial connections or to help you gain acceptance into a particular group. It can be a bonding experience that helps you feel less alone. And it allows you to be judgmental and temporarily feel better about yourself, although usually at the expense of others.

At the same time, gossip is a way to avoid direct contact with your partner – or the person about whom you are gossiping. Unless it leads to personal revelations about you or a deeper sharing between you, the resulting connection is not an intimate one.

And to the extent that it keeps you from connecting with yourself by externalizing your focus on others, it can actually *interfere* with your ability to form an intimate connection with your partner.

Intimacy must be connected back to you.

Intimacy is about allowing your partner to relate to you, which cannot happen if you present yourself in a way that is "out there" and completely disconnected from who you are.

This means bringing a personal element to what you talk about, such as how it affects you, how you feel about it, or how it relates to your own hopes, dreams, fears, expectations or values.

In other words, a conversation is just a conversation unless and until you include some reference back to yourself.

"Of course I care about how you imagined I thought
you perceived I wanted you to feel."

An intimate conversation is about talking with rather than at each other.

Even a seemingly open and honest conversation in which you and your partner are revealing the deepest feelings in the most heartfelt way is not an intimate exchange if each of you is thinking about what you will say next.

Slow down and take in what your partner has shared with you, clarify by asking questions, and check in to see if they feel heard, acknowledged and understood before continuing.

If you are the one who doesn't feel heard or understood, let your partner know specifically what it is you need before you allow the conversation to move on.

Deep listening is miraculous for both listener and speaker. When someone receives us with open-hearted, non-judging, intensely interested listening, our spirits expand.

Sue Patton Thoele

An intimate conversation involves active listening.

Intimacy involves not only listening to your partner but also *active* listening.

Much more than simply repeating back or paraphrasing what was said, active listening includes mirroring, which means reflecting back from your own perspective both the content and the underlying feeling of what your partner is saying. It also includes clarifying by asking questions rather than making interpretations or assuming you already know the answers.

The process of active listening sends the message that what your partner is sharing with you Is important and meaningful, and that you are willing to invest your time and effort to understand it.

You must explicitly state your needs in an intimate relationship.

It is a mistake to assume that just because you are in an intimate relationship and your partner cares about you that they "should" know what you need.

No matter how well your partner knows you or how much they care about you, they have no way of knowing your needs – and there is no chance of your needs being met – unless you are clear and direct in expressing them.

Stating your needs is as important as expressing your feelings. At the same time, you can only ask – not demand or expect – that your needs be met by your partner.

What are your needs...

- For time together?
- For time by yourself?
- For time with other people?
- For communication?
- For understanding?
- For exclusivity?
- For validation?
- For affection?
- For support?
- For help?
- For sex?

Electronic communication can create the illusion of intimacy.

Electronic communication is a medium that encourages intimacy by allowing you to reveal thoughts and feelings that you might not share with anyone else or that you might not be comfortable expressing face-to-face.

But without the benefit of direct face-to-face interaction, electronic communication can also create a false sense of intimacy by providing a screen through which you can reveal as much or as little as you choose, and consciously or unconsciously filter or distort what you reveal. In this way, you end up creating a false persona that may attract other false personas doing exactly the same thing.

Electronic communication is an instantaneous and illusory contact that creates a sense of intimacy without the emotional investment that leads to close friendships.

Clifford Stoll

Electronic communication alone cannot sustain intimacy.

Electronic communication such as email, text messages, Facebook or IM can lay the groundwork for an intimate relationship and be used for maintaining an intimate connection when you and your partner are separated.

But words and emoticons are one-dimensional and are not a substitute for face-to-face interactions, which reveal more of who you are and what you are communicating through your tone of voice, touch, facial expressions and body language.

Keep in mind that words themselves are limiting and reductionistic, and cannot possibly capture the richness and nuance of direct interpersonal contact.

And if you become too reliant on social networks and mobile devices for maintaining your connections, you run the risk of replacing real friends with virtual friends, real contact with virtual contact, and depth with superficiality.

The question then is whether you are using electronic communication as a way to *avoid* intimacy rather than as a way to *enhance* it.

Your choice of words matters in an intimate conversation.

The specific words you choose to express yourself in an intimate relationship can affect how receptive your partner will be to what you have to say.

The differences may seem subtle, but clear "I" statements are much more effective – and less provocative – than "you" statements, "why" questions or absolutes.

"You" statements:

- You make me...
- You need to...
- You should ...
- You can't...
- You're so...

"Why" questions:

- Why are you...
- Why do you...
- Why didn't you...
- Why won't you...
- Why can't you...

Absolutes:

- You always...
- You never...
- Everything...
- Nothing...

"I" statements:

- I feel...
- I am...
- I need...
- I want...
- I think...
- I like...
- I prefer...
- I hear...

Intimacy makes no assumptions.

It is not intimacy to assume that your partner thinks or feels a certain way without first checking it out...

It is not intimacy to project your own thoughts or feelings onto your partner...

It is not intimacy to insist that you know what your partner truly thinks or feels...

It is not intimacy to assert that your partner should think or feel the way you do...

All of these are likely to have less to do with your partner and more to do with your own judgments or fears about what they might be thinking or feeling.

"This isn't really about water. This is about what's going on between us."

Intimacy is as much about process as content.

Content is *what* you are talking about in a conversation, including both thoughts and feelings. Process is *how* you share and receive it.

Process is especially important in the midst of conflict. So even if you view the content of the conflict as negative or unpleasant, the process itself can still be positive and constructive.

You will be more effective at resolving conflict if you and your partner are each aware of your respective feelings, open and congruent in expressing them, and concerned and respectful of those of your partner.

Content:

- Why are you late?
- You kept me waiting for forty-five minutes.
- I wasted my time sitting here waiting for you.
- Couldn't you have called?

Process:

- I get worried when I don't hear from you.
- I'm angry now that I find you're okay.
- I'm annoyed that you didn't call.
- I need to be able to rely on you.

I want to know if you can sit with pain

mine or your own

without moving to hide it

or fade it

or fix it.

Oriah Mountain Dreamer
The Invitation

Sometimes it's okay to just "be" in an intimate relationship.

Talking is one way to express your feelings,
   but sometimes
      the best way to connect with your partner
        is simply to remain silent,
          and feel their presence and companionship.

Conflict is not only the wall, but also the door. Only in passing through the conflict that is virtually inevitable in a relationship are we able to reach the deeper levels of intimacy.

Gary Smalley
Secrets to Lasting Love

Intimacy and Conflict

Any relationship that is important to us – one in which we have a lot at stake in its success – can easily trigger our unresolved issues. If we don't care about someone, we're less easily triggered because it doesn't matter if the relationship works or doesn't work.

Sharon M. Rivkin, M.A., M.F.T.

It's natural to have conflict in an intimate relationship.

Conflict in an intimate relationship means that you and your partner are bumping up against each other's boundaries by being autonomous and separate individuals with different needs, experiences, priorities and interests.

Conflict itself is not a problem; viewing conflict as a problem or being unwilling to work through it in a conscious and constructive way is.

No problem can be solved from the same level of consciousness that created it.

Albert Einstein

Resolving conflict in an intimate relationship is the path to deeper intimacy.

As long as you and your partner are willing to openly discuss conflict and negotiate a solution that works for both of you, conflict provides an opportunity to strengthen an intimate relationship.

Resolving conflict enables you to connect with your partner on a deeper level, to learn more about your partner's feelings and needs, and to become more aware of and communicate your own.

Conflict resolution strategy:

- Respond rather than react.
- Summarize the issue in neutral terms.
- Identify specifically what is important to you.
- Explicitly express your feelings and needs.
- Acknowledge and actively listen to your partner.
- Be flexible in your thinking.
- Use short and concise statements.
- Avoid bringing up the past.
- Make requests, not demands.
- Focus on observations, not interpretations.
- Take turns talking for a minute at a time.
- Be patient with the process and with each other.
- Work towards a mutually acceptable solution.

Love me when I least deserve it,
because that's when I need it most

Swedish Proverb

You will inevitably be disappointed and hurt in an intimate relationship.

Because you and your partner are distinct individuals, you will at some point be disappointed or hurt by your partner. This is not an indication that something is wrong with you, your partner or the relationship, or that your partner does not care about you.

You simply can't please each other nor satisfy each other's needs all of the time.

The irony of intimacy is that those with whom we are closest are also those most able to disappoint and hurt us or to reactivate our old wounds. More importantly, they are the ones who can help us to heal them.

The point here is not whether you will be disappointed or hurt but how you express it when you are, how your partner receives it, how the two of you navigate your way through it, and what you learn about yourself and each other through the process.

The less you open your heart to others,
the more your heart suffers.

Deepak Chopra

Intimacy involves a commitment to working things out.

Commitment in an intimate relationship includes a willingness to constructively work through conflicts and other challenges with your partner until they are resolved without becoming fed up, shutting down, running away, or avoiding them all together.

At the same time, an issue or conflict that cycles again and again or a negative pattern of interaction that keeps recurring may call for a new way of listening, a change in perspective or behavior, or the help of an objective third party.

In those cases where you've tried and failed to resolve a particular challenge, sometimes the goal is simply to achieve additional clarity, learn something new about yourself, and revisit the issue with a fresh perspective at a later time.

And if the relationship ends, view it not as a failure but rather as a learning experience and an opportunity to transition into a new way of being.

It is very important for every human being to forgive herself or himself because if you live, you will make mistakes – it is inevitable. But once you do and you see the mistake, then you forgive yourself and say, 'Well, if I'd known better I'd have done better,' that's all. So you say to people who you think you may have injured, 'I'm sorry,' and then you say to yourself, 'I'm sorry.' If we all hold on to the mistake, we can't see our own glory in the mirror because we have the mistake between our faces and the mirror; we can't see what we're capable of being. You can ask forgiveness of others, but in the end the real forgiveness is in one's own self.

Maya Angelou

We all make mistakes in our intimate relationships.

When you make a mistake, you must be willing to acknowledge it, take responsibility for it, and work through it until both you and your partner have a sense of closure.

When your partner makes a mistake, acknowledges it, takes responsibility for it, and you both have a sense of closure, you must ultimately be willing to forgive it.

The delicate balance here is that while keeping unresolved issues to yourself can be harmful to an intimate relationship, bringing up past issues again and again can be equally harmful.

Resolution may take a lot of work and patience, but without a willingness to forgive your partner – and yourself – it is virtually impossible to heal, move forward, and put the past behind you.

Forgiveness is key in an intimate relationship.

Forgiving your partner in an intimate relationship may be difficult or even seem impossible if you feel betrayed, when the tendency is to further victimize yourself by asking, "How could you have done that to me if you cared about me?"

The challenge of forgiveness is sometimes to be willing to look at how you may have helped to co-create the situation, how you may have been part of the process, and how you may have contributed to the circumstances that led to the hurtful outcome.

This is not to say that you are responsible or to blame for your partner's behavior but rather to help you understand how it was something that happened *between* you rather than *to* you.

The bottom line is that every situation is one that we help to co-create, in which we are a participant, and for which we bear at least some of the responsibility. So the task may be to not only forgive your partner but also forgive yourself.

Intimacy is being seen and known
as the person you truly are.

Amy Bloom

Intimacy is not about pretending that everything is fine.

Intimacy is about sharing your internal world rather than concealing it just to be "nice," please your partner, maintain the status quo, or avoid rocking the boat.

If you indicate that you are "fine" when you are not, insist that "nothing" is wrong when something is bothering you, or express your feelings using words, tone and body language that are not congruent with your internal state, you create a disconnect not only within yourself but also between you and your partner.

Sex can be used as a way to avoid intimacy.

Sex becomes less fulfilling and nourishing over time when used as an alternative to dealing with unresolved issues or conflicts, either within the relationship or within yourself.

Emotional intimacy, by contrast, provides the foundation to work through these issues and conflicts, enables you to stay connected in the long-term, and enhances sexual intimacy.

When we trust ourselves, we become more humble and more daring. When we trust ourselves, we move surely. There is no unnecessary strain in our grasp as we reach out to meet life. There is no snatching at people and events, trying to force them to give us what we think we want. We become what we are meant to be. It is that simple. We become what we are, and we do it by being who we are, not who we strive to be.

Julia Cameron
The Sound of Paper: Starting from Scratch

Intimacy is remaining receptive when you most want to shut down.

It is relatively easy to be open to issues that have nothing to do with you or the relationship. The real challenge of intimacy is to remain open when your partner shares feelings and perceptions that you view as negative or with which you can't identify, especially those that involve and are directed at you.

Even if your partner views you as the source of their pain, you feel attacked or blamed, or it feels uncomfortable, intimacy requires that you be the one with whom your partner can talk about it.

This does not mean that you must agree – sometimes all your partner needs is to feel heard – but simply that you remain open and receptive rather than becoming defensive and shutting down.

Our emotions act as a radar. Through them we experience the world around us and gather information about it. They detect "blips" in our world, they produce "intelligence" about what is happening around us and they filter this "intelligence" back to the thinking parts of our brain. These feelings, or intuitions, are then communicated to the brain where we make decisions about how to react.

Kellen Von Houser

There's nothing wrong with anger in an intimate relationship.

Like any feeling, anger is both informative and transient. And it needs an outlet. It only becomes problematic when it's held onto or destructively acted out.

Within an intimate relationship, anger needs to be both expressed and received constructively.

Expressing anger means simply stating it without yelling, attacking, blaming, becoming aggressive, or engaging in passive-aggressive behavior.

Receiving anger means being willing to hear your partner's anger in a non-defensive, non-reactive and empathic way.

Angry feelings are not a problem. Angry *behavior* is.

It's a lot easier to be angry at someone than it is to tell them you're hurt.

Tom Gates

In an intimate relationship, anger can often mask other feelings.

As important as it is to express and receive anger in an intimate relationship, recognize that other feelings – hurt, sadness, fear, shame, frustration or helplessness – often lie beneath it.

If you or your partner is angry, step back and consider whether the anger may be concealing any underlying, more vulnerable feelings.

At the same time, ask yourself whether there may be some old pattern of outdated or unexamined thoughts that are fueling the feelings.

Once you are able to look beneath the surface, you and your partner have an opportunity to discover unknown parts of yourselves, and to heal those parts you may not even have known were wounded.

Resentment is like drinking poison and waiting for the other person to die.

Carrie Fisher

Resentment is destructive to intimacy.

If you harbor resentment and keep it pent up inside, you will feel less connected with and become hardened towards your partner, and you may also suffer negative health consequences.

Once the feelings underlying the resentment are expressed by you – and heard non-defensively by your partner – resentment will often dissipate.

You will then have an opportunity to reconnect with your partner and move forward rather than continuing to live in the past

When you plant lettuce, if it does not grow well, you don't blame the lettuce. You look for reasons it is not doing well. It may need fertilizer, or more water, or less sun. You never blame the lettuce.

Yet if we have problems with our friends or our family, we blame the other person. But if we know how to take care of them, they will grow well, like the lettuce. Blaming has no positive effect at all, nor does trying to persuade using reason and argument. That is my experience. If you understand, and you show that you understand, you can love, and the situation will change.

Thich Nhat Hanh

Intimacy requires that you actively engage in conflict resolution.

Resolving conflict includes a willingness to engage in the process in a meaningful way.

This means being open to hearing and expressing both sides of a conflict, hanging in there until each of you feels heard and is ready to move on, and focusing on a solution that works for both of you.

Attempting to avoid conflict or simply going through the motions with automated responses sends the message that you are closed off and aren't interested in working through the issues constructively.

More than simply being *willing* to work things out, this is about *how* you work things out.

Conflict avoidance statements:

- Can't we just drop it?
- Forget I even said anything.
- Never mind.
- I don't care anymore.

Automated responses:

- Okay.
- Fine.
- Whatever.
- It doesn't matter.

SIPRESS

"Well, if it doesn't matter who's right and who's wrong, why don't I be right and you be wrong?"

Intimacy is not dismissive, attacking, defensive or invalidating.

Programmed responses that are dismissive, attacking, defensive or invalidating suggest that you are closed off and not open to intimacy or learning anything new about yourself.

Dismissive:

- Can't you just let it go?
- Do we have to keep talking about this?
- Fine, it's all me.

Attacking:

- You never…
- Why didn't you…
- Why can't you ever…

Defensive:

- You know how I am.
- No one else has ever told me that.
- But I didn't do anything wrong.

Invalidating:

- You're too sensitive.
- You're being irrational.
- You shouldn't feel that way.

The moment we close the door on one or more aspects of ourselves, we set into motion a secret life… Our unresolved shame causes us to act out; it eventually gets expressed as an outer behavior that blows the cover off the parts of our life we've been trying to conceal. We can work day and night trying to control our hidden impulses from ever coming to the surface, but we are only a moment away from acting out in ways that undermine our self-respect.

Debbie Ford
The Shadow Effect

Acting out is a way to avoid intimacy.

Acting out by engaging in behaviors that you know will hurt your partner – or violate either a personal or relationship boundary – is destructive to you, your partner, and the relationship.

Acting out also precludes you and your partner from addressing and resolving conflicts within the relationship or feelings within yourself.

Acting out:

- Lacks self-control.
- Often unconscious.
- Typically harmful or destructive.
- Expresses unacceptable impulses.
- Provides short-term relief from anxiety.
- Inhibits more constructive approaches.

"If you were my husband, I would poison your tea."

Lady Astor

"Madam, if you were my wife, I would drink it!"

Winston Churchill

Intimacy requires that you trust your partner's intentions.

Trust within an intimate relationship includes trusting that your partner's motives are good. It means giving your partner the benefit of the doubt rather than viewing them through a negative filter and attributing to them an intent to deceive, manipulate, control or hurt you.

If you are in doubt about your partner's intentions, check them out either by asking or simply stating your observations. Otherwise, you risk interpreting them incorrectly, and may be imposing your own projections or mistrust onto your partner.

Intimacy is not a referendum.

Quoting other people who agree with your point of view is provocative, puts your partner on the defensive, and only serves to make you right and your partner wrong. It is also an indication that you are focusing on thoughts and opinions rather than on the underlying feelings.

Quoting other people is unnecessary because your feelings are always valid, as are your partner's. This is true even if you think you would not feel the same way under similar circumstances, and even if you believe that a hundred other people – or the rest of the world – could not possibly feel what your partner is feeling in a particular situation.

The bottom line is that it doesn't matter what people outside of your relationship think or feel, so be direct about your own feelings and experience – and accepting of those of your partner – and leave everyone else out of the discussion.

Intimacy sometimes requires that you take a breath.

When you become stuck, rigid or polarized, caught up in a battle for control, or entrenched in a position that prevents you from seeing the broader context...

When you find yourself overly focused on or distancing yourself from your partner, talking too much or remaining totally silent, or venting a lot of negative feelings or content...

When the process itself has broken down, has intense energy around it, is becoming circular or repetitive, is escalating in tone or volume, or seems to be taking on a life of its own...

When your interactions have become alienating rather than healing, or you are attributing the negative aspects of your interactions to your partner...

It may be a good time to slow down, step back, drop deeper into yourself, and let your partner know that you need some time to think and get more perspective before proceeding.

It's impossible to fail at anything. Your success just may not look the way you thought it would.

Byron Katie
A Thousand Names for Joy

Intimacy always involves the risk of loss.

The honesty associated with intimacy is risky. You or your partner may reveal or discover something that creates an insurmountable impasse, where you must compromise a core value or your own personal integrity in order to stay in the relationship.

Having intimacy does not necessarily mean that the relationship can be saved, or even that it should be saved. Only you can decide whether it's healthier for you to be in or out of the relationship. But it is better to lose a relationship than to try to save it at the expense of yourself and your well-being.

Instead of faulting your partner and walking away from the relationship angry, with judgment and blame, or needing to be right, you can choose to learn from the experience. You can then carry positive lessons into the next relationship rather than repeat negative patterns again and again.

Having clarity and resolution through honesty will serve your own growth regardless of whether or not the relationship survives.

Oh, the miraculous energy that flows between two people who care enough to get beyond surfaces and games, who are willing to take the risks of being totally open, of listening, of responding with the whole heart. How much we can do for each other.

Alex Noble

Challenges of Intimacy

It takes courage… to endure the sharp pains of self-discovery rather than choose to take the dull pain of unconsciousness that would last the rest of our lives.

Marianne Williamson
A Return to Love

Intimacy takes courage.

In an intimate relationship...

It takes courage to be imperfect, look within, see your own flaws, and stay focused on your own issues rather than those of your partner.

It takes courage to surrender your ego, fully reveal yourself, stand emotionally naked in front of your partner, and be seen completely as you are.

It takes courage to express your true feelings, be vulnerable, risk being hurt, and expose your authentic self when it might lead to conflict or loss.

It takes courage to believe in yourself enough to speak up, express your needs, state your truth, and stand up for yourself.

It takes courage to connect.

and...

It takes courage to change.

Being right gets in the way of intimacy.

Attempting to be right in an intimate relationship is often about gaining power and control, and is all about your ego. It closes you off from learning anything new and can alienate your partner.

Even if you think you are right, your partner may be equally right from their point of view, since each of you may actually be seeing or experiencing the same thing from a different perspective.

Keep in mind that there is rarely one objective truth about anything. If you insist on being right, you make your partner wrong, and you, your partner and your relationship will all suffer.

Fear can be a barrier to intimacy.

Fear can prevent you from taking the emotional risks necessary to build and maintain an intimate relationship.

Fear can be based on past hurts, disappointments, betrayals or judgments, and may include the fear of losing the relationship or of losing yourself in the relationship.

Having fears is not necessarily a barrier to intimacy, but a lack of consciousness around them or an unwillingness to share them with your partner is.

I cannot always control what goes on outside.
But I can always control what goes on inside.

Wayne Dyer

Intimacy is unpredictable.

Intimacy involves another person over whom you have no control. You cannot control your partner's feelings, perceptions or behavior, nor their experience of you, others, or the world at large.

All you can control is how you respond and interact with your partner and the level of intimacy you share by remaining open and receptive to what happens both within you and between you.

If you find yourself attempting to take control in your relationship, it may be an indication that you are carrying around some underlying fears.

Intimacy is not competitive.

Being competitive may satisfy the needs of your individual ego but it is likely to do so at the expense of your partner and the relationship.

In a competitive relationship, you are working against each other and only one of you can win.

An intimate relationship is about working together and alongside each other – in a cooperative, supportive and encouraging way – so that you and your partner can *both* win.

Intimacy is not codependency.

Intimacy is interdependent, where each of you is separate, whole, and able to move freely between dependence and independence within the relationship.

It is not about seeking the love and approval of your partner at the expense of yourself, attempting to control your partner's behavior by doing for them what they are able to do for themselves, or allowing yourself to be controlled by your partner out of fear of anger, rejection or abandonment.

Codependency:

- Overly focused on partner.
- Addicted to the relationship.
- Self-destructive.
- Excessively self-sacrificing.
- Compromising your own values.
- Unable to set healthy boundaries.
- Assumes role of rescuer or martyr.
- Absorbing your partner's problems.
- Too attached to a specific outcome.
- Behavior driven by guilt or shame.
- Unhealthy emotional dependency.
- Needing to please in order to feel whole.

The more deeply and honestly you love, and the more trust you create between you, the more your partner and your relationship will confront you with the truth, and the more uncomfortable you may become! It is at these times when you need to find the courage to stay instead of running, the courage to move into the truth instead of away from it, the courage to remain open instead of closing off – the courage to keep loving.

Barbara De Angelis, Ph.D.
Real Moments for Lovers

Addiction is a barrier to intimacy.

Addiction to alcohol, drugs, pornography, gambling or sex – or any other compulsive behavior – can interfere with your ability to establish and maintain intimacy. Left untreated, addiction will result in alienation, isolation, and the deterioration of your relationships.

If you have a close relationship to someone with an addiction, be aware of your own desire to fix the problem – you can't – as well as behavior that, while well-intentioned, may lead to a codependent relationship. Codependency can itself become an addiction when you compulsively focus on "helping" your partner to the detriment of yourself.

If you find yourself in either position, consider seeking professional help or a 12-step program.

Relationships – of all kinds – are like sand held in your hand. Held loosely, with an open hand, the sand remains where it is. The minute you close your hand and squeeze tightly to hold on, the sand trickles through your fingers. You may hold onto some of it, but most will be spilled. A relationship is like that. Held loosely, with respect and freedom for the other person, it is likely to remain intact. But hold too tightly, too possessively, and the relationship slips away and is lost.

Kaleel Jamison

Intimacy does not come naturally to everyone.

Few of us have had good or even adequate role models for intimacy, nor is it taught, encouraged or reinforced within our culture.

Intimacy can be unfamiliar, a struggle, and even seem impossible at times, particularly under stressful circumstances or in anxiety-provoking situations, and the process itself typically breaks down.

Until you decide to break unexamined and often reactive patterns of relating that don't work, and get in touch with the more vulnerable feelings that lie beneath your defenses, you can't begin the journey towards greater personal awareness and deeper, more intimate relationships.

"I'm not quite ready yet. Why don't you come in and make us a drink while I figure out how not to project all my hopes and fears onto you?"

Intimacy is realistic.

Intimacy is not about finding perfection; it's about accepting imperfection. Neither your partner nor your relationship is perfect – nor are you.

Putting your partner on a pedestal, projecting onto them your own expectations, or assuming the relationship will be conflict-free are all unrealistic and will lead to disappointment and even resentment down the line.

Seeing your partner as they are rather than seeing only what you want to see – and embracing the whole person rather than just a part – is vital to creating and sustaining intimacy.

"Maybe it was your childhood, Spike, but most guys find it hard to be intimate..."

Intimacy includes a willingness to challenge old patterns and beliefs.

Intimacy includes a willingness to change old patterns of relating that no longer work for you – including reactivity that may be rooted in unresolved conflict or feelings from past relationships – as well as an openness to learning and practicing new relationship skills.

This begins with an awareness of your own relationship history and how it may be negatively affecting your current relationships. It includes looking at your beliefs and assumptions about relationships – including those around stereotypical male and female roles within a relationship.

It also includes examining your family history with respect to conflict – how it was resolved, how feelings were or were not expressed and received, the "should" and "shouldn't" messages within your family, and how family members treated each other during times of stress.

"I know. But I think I can change him."

Intimacy is not about changing your partner.

Attempting to change your partner in an intimate relationship will result in a battle for control that will ultimately lead to disappointment, frustration and resentment. It is also a sign of codependence.

You cannot determine for your partner what needs to change or when those changes need to occur.

You can only make changes within yourself through an awareness of and willingness to shift your own thoughts, feelings and behaviors, and only when you are ready to delve deeper into yourself. This includes examining the discomfort that underlies your desire to change your partner.

It is through these changes – and changing how you choose to interact with your partner – that change within the relationship is possible.

I'm sorry, John, but that wasn't the real me then. That was the me that was trying to get you to like me.
machlis

Intimacy has its limits.

Intimacy is a lot of things but…

It cannot make you feel okay
if you do not feel okay about yourself.

It cannot make you feel good
if you do not feel good about yourself.

If cannot make you feel trust
if you do not trust yourself.

It cannot make you feel accepted
if you do not accept yourself.

It cannot make you feel secure
if you are not secure within yourself.

It cannot make you feel fulfilled
if your life is not fulfilling.

It cannot make you feel seen
if you are not willing to see all of who you are.

It cannot make you feel loved
if you do not already love yourself.

and…

It cannot always save your relationship.

A woman marries a man expecting he will change, but he doesn't.

A man marries a woman expecting that she won't change, and she does.

Unknown

Intimacy Over Time

Passion is the quickest to develop, and the quickest to fade. Intimacy develops more slowly, and commitment more gradually still.

Robert Sternberg

Intimacy begins after the initial euphoria of a new relationship ends.

The intense feelings you experience in the early stages of an intimate relationship don't last, no matter how special or different you think the relationship is nor how strong the connection appears to be.

Many relationships don't survive the transition from blissful infatuation to the more challenging stages of building a lasting relationship. Rather than working through the post-infatuation stage, you or your partner may simply cut and run for another "love shot" by moving on to the excitement of the next new relationship.

But the upside of hanging in there after the initial rush begins to fade is that you will have a chance to develop deeper intimacy, to become more whole, and to experience a level of connection that occurs only in the context of a long-term relationship rather than a series of short-term ones.

GOOD WILL HUNTING

WILL HUNTING (Matt Damon)
This girl's like, you know, beautiful. She's smart, she's
fun, she's different from most of the girls I've been with...

SEAN MAGUIRE (Robin Williams)
So call her up, Romeo.

WILL
Why? So I can realize she's not that smart, that she's
f--king boring. I mean, you know, this girl's like
f--king perfect right now. I don't want to ruin that.

SEAN
Maybe you're perfect right now, maybe you don't want
to ruin that.
        (Will says nothing.)
Well, I think that's a super philosophy Will. That
way you can go through your entire life without ever
having to really know anybody.
        (Sean talks about his late wife.)
People call these things imperfections, but they're not.
Aw, that's the good stuff. And then we get to choose
who we let into our weird little worlds. You're not
perfect sport. And let me save you the suspense. This
girl you met; she isn't perfect either. But the question
is whether or not you're perfect for each other. That's
the whole deal. That's what intimacy is all about.

Intimacy is about making the transition from ideal to real.

The excitement, optimism and mutual acceptance that fuel the development of intimacy at the beginning of a relationship are typically based upon you and your partner presenting yourselves – and seeing each other – in the best possible light.

It's natural to want to hold onto this state because you are not only seeing an idealized version of your partner but also seeing in their reflection an idealized version of yourself – a pleasant one-dimensional illusion that can't be sustained.

As additional dimensions of who you are begin to surface and you become more real to each other, each of you is confronted by the reality of two less-than-perfect individuals in a less-than-perfect relationship and risks being rejected or abandoned by the other.

Accepting and embracing this imperfect reality is a key turning point in every relationship. The challenge is to confront the fear of exposing the full truth of who you are and consciously let go of the idealizations about your partner and yourself.

It's your willingness to experience vulnerability, face your fear of abandonment or engulfment, and embrace a more whole view of yourself and your partner that leads to genuine intimacy, a richer relationship, and a more authentic life.

"I don't have time to talk about this now. Can't it wait until we're dead?"

Intimacy requires ongoing effort.

Being open to your partner is relatively easy in the early "getting-to-know-you" stages of your relationship.

But as the novelty of a new relationship wears off, the initial excitement fades, and you and your partner become more predictable to each other, you both face the challenge of keeping the relationship passionate, nourishing and alive.

Maintaining a spirit of openness, curiosity and gratitude over time enables you to stay connected, and keeps your relationship fresh as each of you changes and grows.

THE THOMAS CROWN AFFAIR

PSYCHIATRIST (Faye Dunaway)
Enjoyment isn't intimacy.

THOMAS CROWN (Pierce Brosnan)
And intimacy isn't necessarily enjoyment.

Intimacy picks up where sex leaves off.

You may think that sex is the most important part of an intimate relationship, and it may seem that way when the relationship is in its honeymoon phase, physical chemistry is powerful, and there is very little conflict between you and your partner.

But over time, it is the deeper connection, communication and sharing of emotional intimacy rather than great sex that will sustain the relationship as conflicts arise and the intensity and frequency of sex inevitably decline.

And while sex may be one way to connect or reconnect in the short-term, it is emotional intimacy that will keep your sex life alive and passionate in the long-term rather than the other way around.

"If you don't like it you can always use it as another example
of how I have no idea who you really are."

Intimacy is not a constant state of being.

Intimacy is fluid and tends to ebb and flow over the course of a relationship. So there will be times when the connection between you and your partner doesn't feel as strong or as close as it once was.

This is inevitable. As you and your partner become more real and get to know each other more fully, the nature of your interactions and the level on which you interact will change and shift.

It can be a challenge for you or your partner to adapt to these changes and for the relationship to find a new equilibrium, especially if either of you resists, feels discomfort, chases after the other, or hits an edge and pulls back.

But by flexibly adapting to these natural shifts rather than rigidly resisting them – and sharing your observations and feelings about them with your partner – you have an opportunity to grow personally as well as deepen the connection between you.

It's not easy being in a relationship, much less to truly know the other one and accept them as they are with all their flaws and baggage. Jack confessed to me his fear of being rejected if I truly knew him, if he showed himself totally bare to me. Jack realized after two years of being with me that he didn't know me at all, nor did I know him. And to truly love each other we needed to know the truth about each other even if it's not so easy to take.

Marion *(Julie Delpy)*
2 Days in Paris

Intimacy is not about being completely aligned.

In the early stages of an intimate relationship, your own individual interests and needs may seem less important than your desire to be together. Either they recede into the background as you and your partner focus more on shared interests and on building the relationship, or you simply neglect them in favor of those of your partner.

In both cases, this early alignment can be misleading and may create an unrealistic set of expectations for yourself, your partner, and the relationship. More importantly, it cannot be sustained over time, especially if one or both of you has initially surrendered a part of yourself to be in the relationship.

And when you and your partner inevitably start refocusing on yourselves – including your need for separateness and autonomy – it may feel hurtful or seem like a problem with the relationship. What matters here is not that you remain completely aligned but that you understand and accept that this is a natural progression in healthy relationships.

People think a soul mate is your perfect fit, and that's what everyone wants. But a true soul mate is a mirror, the person who shows you everything that is holding you back, the person who brings you to your own attention so you can change your life.

Elizabeth Gilbert
Eat, Pray, Love

Maintaining a spirit of openness allows intimacy to grow.

The early stages of an intimate relationship are usually marked by optimism, enthusiasm and excitement. It's a time of exploration and discovery when your guard is down and you and your partner are open and receptive to each other.

At some point, however, you may find that you are becoming resistant to or defended against learning anything new about your partner or exploring parts of yourself that you don't want to see. Your tendency may be to pull back, close off, or become controlling.

What underlies resistance and defensiveness is often fear of abandonment, engulfment, rejection, or loss of control. These fears may surface as you become more emotionally invested in the relationship, experience power shifts between you and your partner, or begin to see the less ego-enhancing parts of yourself reflected back to you through your partner.

Your reaction may be to avoid and conceal your fears rather than acknowledge and share them. But by moving into your vulnerability, staying with your feelings, and expressing as clearly as possible what's happening within you, you create an opportunity for self-discovery and personal growth, renewed openness, and deeper connection with your partner.

At first, it was the real thing, and sheer delight. It is the part of the relationship in which you are at your best: fun, charming, excited, exciting, interesting, interested. It is a time when you're most comfortable and lovable because you do not feel the need to mobilize your defenses, so your partner gets to cuddle a warm human being instead of a giant cactus. It is a time of delight for both, and it's no wonder you like openings so much you strive to make your life a series of them.

But beginnings cannot be prolonged endlessly; they cannot simply state and restate and restate themselves. They must move on and develop – or die of boredom.

Richard Bach
The Bridge Across Forever

When intimacy breaks down, your interactions with your partner will become more negative.

When you find that you are unwilling to share the more vulnerable parts of yourself or are focusing more on the negative aspects of your partner and the relationship, it's likely that the intimate connection between you and your partner is deteriorating.

It may also be an indication that you've become disconnected from yourself.

This is an opportunity to explore what may be going on beneath the surface, to get in touch with your underlying feelings, to reflect on how you may be contributing to the breakdown in your relationship, and to openly share this process with your partner.

It's also a time to reassess and focus on the more positive aspects of your relationship and what brought you and your partner together in the first place, to reevaluate what's most important to you, and to learn more about yourself.

And keep in mind that your partner's negative characteristics are intricately linked to the positive ones – as are yours.

When you are offended at any man's fault, turn to yourself and study your own failings. Then you will forget your anger.

Epictetus

What initially attracts you to your intimate partner may also drive you apart.

What initially attracted you to your partner in the early stages of your relationship can soon become what triggers, irritates or even repels you.

Every strength or "positive" quality has an opposite or "shadow" side. The shadow qualities – those parts of you that are selfish, controlling, unworthy, demanding, manipulative, entitled – are easier to spot in your partner than in yourself.

When you are willing to see that these parts also exist within you and you are able to own and embrace rather than judge or deny them – or project them onto your partner – you connect more fully to yourself and your partner.

And the more you can embrace your dualistic nature and the often paradoxical aspects of yourself, the more whole you will become, and the more capable you will be of deep and fulfilling intimacy.

When Freudian slips reveal a
less-than-perfect relationship.

A positive balance is essential for lasting intimacy.

Positive interactions come easily and naturally in the early stages of an intimate relationship. But over time, as you become more familiar and comfortable with each other, it takes more of an intentional effort to ensure that the positive continues to outweigh the negative.

Often this can be as simple as letting your partner know what it is that you like about them, that you are grateful that they chose you, and how much you appreciate having them in your life.

Try to make positive exchanges between you and your partner a daily practice. Be creative. Make an effort to learn how and when your partner feels most appreciated – and then act on it.

Positive expressions:

- A smile.
- A compliment.
- A kind gesture.
- A playful remark.
- A simple thank you.
- An encouraging word.
- A thoughtful gift or note.
- An embrace or gentle touch.
- Recalling a fond memory you share.
- Acknowledging positive change or growth.

Change is inevitable in an intimate relationship.

Change can be uncomfortable and even frightening because it means letting go of what's familiar and predictable.

In order to sustain an intimate relationship and grow personally, you must adapt to healthy changes in your partner and the relationship. You must also be willing to change your own unhealthy behaviors and patterns of interacting.

Being open to change, remaining flexible, maintaining a spirit of curiosity, staying in touch with your vulnerability, speaking your truth, and finding new approaches that work for both of you will allow you and your partner to grow with each other – and your relationship to flourish.

One generation plants the trees,
and another gets the shade.

Chinese Proverb

You can affect future generations through your intimate relationships.

Even if your own upbringing was less than optimal and you have a history of unsuccessful relationships, you can still choose a different path.

With effort, practice and reinforcement in the context of an intimate relationship, you can change the way you view and relate to yourself and those around you.

Even seemingly small shifts in your behavior and how you relate can have a profound impact on all of your relationships.

It won't happen overnight but if you are committed and willing to do the work, you have the power to change not only your own life but also the lives of others by providing a healthy model for intimacy.

This includes not only a direct effect on those in your immediate circle but also an indirect effect through the chain of relationships on people you don't even know, including future generations over time.

Some of the biggest challenges in relationships come from the fact that most people enter a relationship in order to get something: they're trying to find someone who's going to make them feel good.

In reality, the only way a relationship will last is if you see your relationship as a place that you go to give, and not a place that you go to take.

Anthony Robbins

Appendices

Look at the weaknesses of others with compassion, not accusation. It's not what they're not doing or should be doing that's the issue. The issue is your own chosen response to the situation and what you should be doing. If you start to think the problem is "out there," stop yourself. That thought is the problem.

Stephen R. Covey
The 7 Habits of Highly Effective People

Summary

- Intimacy is about connecting in your personal relationships.

- Emotional connection is the long-term glue that binds.

- It takes a willing partner to have an intimate relationship.

- The most important relationship you have is with yourself.

- Awareness and courage are essential for connection.

- Keep your ego in check in your personal relationships.

- Get out of your head and into your heart.

- Keep coming back to yourself and your feelings and needs.

- Drop your defenses and be vulnerable.

- Process is as important as content.

- Tone and body language are as important as words.

- Your partner will often trigger your own issues.

- Conflict is an opportunity rather than a problem.

- Respect individual needs, boundaries and differences.

- Be aware of your fears and projections.

- Being right creates a winner and a loser.

- Change takes time and requires effort and practice.

- The only person you can change is yourself.

- The people around you will be influenced by changes in you.

Only when we are comfortable with who we are can we truly function independently in a healthy way, can we truly function within a relationship.

Two halves do not make a whole when it comes to a healthy relationship: it takes two wholes.

Patricia Fry

Epilogue

The process of writing this book challenged us in some surprising ways, exposing the rough edges of our relationship that still needed polishing, and in some cases, forcing us to confront and refine our respective ideas about intimacy in a relationship.

Challenges that we encountered included external sources of stress, differences in style and approach, conflicting needs and priorities, and ultimately, challenges around process. Not surprisingly, these are the same tripping points found in every relationship.

At various times, one or both of us openly questioned our ability to successfully work together when we fell back into old negative patterns of relating and struggled to resolve conflict.

What brought us back together each time was one of us managing to step out of an external focus and into an internal one, out of the content and into the process, out of our heads and into our hearts, and out of judgment and into vulnerability – the very insights about which we were writing.

This process underscored the fact that even with awareness and a deep level of connection, we still falter, and no doubt will continue to falter in our relationships with each other and others. But we're each a work in progress and we persevere.

Intimacy is a never-ending journey with many bumps in the road and barriers to overcome, but it is a journey well-worth taking because there are so many little treasures to be had along the way. And the beauty of the journey is that at any given time, we can choose a new direction where the landscape is different, there's new growth, and we can see alternative views and perspectives.

Sue and Paul ☺

What **Now**

Now that you've finished this book, you might be eager for more, not sure what to do next, and asking yourself, "Where do I go from here?" In other words, awareness is a good start, but how do you incorporate all of the insights into your life and put them into action? What specific things can you do on a daily basis to increase the level of intimacy in your relationships? And how can you strengthen your connection with yourself and others by being more clear about your feelings and needs?

Here are 20 practical steps to get you started immediately:

1. Reach out to a family member simply to tell them that you love them.

2. Let a friend know that you appreciate them being in your life and why.

3. In a romantic relationship, start a dialogue about the difference between your sexual needs and your emotional needs.

4. Build a better connection with yourself – and those around you – by saying how you feel rather than what you think.

5. The next time you want to reach out to someone, make a phone call instead of sending an email or text.

6. To explore the potential for a deeper relationship with someone new, invite them to coffee or tea in a quiet location.

7. The next time you're asked how you're doing, open up a bit and describe your internal state rather than simply responding, "Great" or "Fine." Be personal and specific.

8. When you want to resolve a conflict, pick up the phone or meet face-to-face rather than sending an email or text.

9. Instead of posting a public comment on a friend's Facebook wall, send them a private message that is more personal.

10. Be willing to express your needs and preferences with friends, family members, in a group, or with your romantic partner.

11. Rather than complain, let your partner know it would mean a lot to you for them to help you in a specific way.

12. During your personal conversations, pay attention to *how* you are communicating in addition to *what* you are saying.

13. The next time you have a conflict, be the first to own and express your part in helping to create it.

14. Notice each time you judge someone and ask yourself how that judgment keeps you from connecting with them.

15. Ask clarifying questions instead of making assumptions or thinking you know what others are thinking or feeling.

16. Stop blaming, criticizing and complaining. Start taking personal responsibility for what's not working and change it.

17. Do something kind for someone you care about without expecting anything in return.

18. Remember to make eye contact in all of your face-to-face interactions.

19. Take a technology "timeout" by turning off your mobile device the next time you are with a friend.

20. Pay attention and try to learn something new about your partner – and yourself – in every interaction you have.

Most importantly, embrace not only those around you, but also yourself – who you are, what you feel, what you need, and what makes you uniquely you. Only by being your authentic self can you have authentic connections and authentic relationships.

Emotional intelligence is the ability to monitor one's own and others' feelings and emotions, to discriminate among them, and to use this information to guide one's thinking and actions.

Peter Salovey and John D. Mayer
Imagination, Cognition, and Personality

Emotional **Intelligence**

No book about emotional intimacy in personal relationships would be complete without at least a mention of the significance of emotional intelligence.

The term *emotional intelligence* – as originally defined on the facing page – was first popularized in mainstream culture by Daniel Goleman in his best-selling book of the same name.

In his book, Goleman introduces the idea that emotional intelligence is as important as – if not more important than – the traditional types of mathematical and verbal intelligence for success in life.

At the very least, emotional intelligence – and the competencies necessary for developing it – provide the necessary foundation on which intimacy is built. Paradoxically, intimate relationships provide an opportunity to further develop and master the competencies of emotional intelligence.

Competencies of emotional intelligence:
- Self-awareness.
- Impulse control.
- Regulating emotions.
- Self-motivation.
- Empathy.
- Attunement.
- Managing relationships.
- Non-defensive listening.
- Soothing yourself and your partner.
- Seeing your partner's point of view.

Feelings

Many of us have a limited vocabulary when it comes to expressing our feelings. The following list is neither exhaustive nor definitive but can help you better identify and express your internal state. The list includes feelings you may have when your needs *are* being met and feelings you may have when your needs are *not* being met.

Feelings when your needs are being met...

Affectionate
compassionate
friendly
loving
open hearted
sympathetic
tender
warm

Engaged
absorbed
alert
curious
engrossed
enchanted
entranced
fascinated
interested
intrigued
involved
spellbound
stimulated

Hopeful
expectant
encouraged
optimistic

Confident
empowered
open
proud
safe
secure

Excited
amazed
animated
ardent
aroused
astonished
dazzled
eager
energetic
enthusiastic
giddy
invigorated
lively
passionate
surprised
vibrant

Grateful
appreciative
moved
thankful
touched

Inspired
amazed
awed
wonder

Joyful
amused
delighted
glad
happy
jubilant
pleased
tickled

Exhilarated
blissful
ecstatic
elated
enthralled
exuberant
radiant
rapturous
thrilled

Peaceful
calm
clear headed
comfortable
centered
content
equanimous
fulfilled
mellow
quiet
relaxed
relieved
satisfied
serene
still
tranquil
trusting

Refreshed
enlivened
rejuvenated
renewed
rested
restored
revived

© 2005 by Center for Nonviolent Communication; www.cnvc.org; cnvc@cnvc.org; 505-244-4041

Feelings when your needs are not being met...

Afraid
apprehensive
dread
foreboding
frightened
mistrustful
panicked
petrified
scared
suspicious
terrified
wary
worried

Annoyed
aggravated
dismayed
disgruntled
displeased
exasperated
frustrated
impatient
irritated
irked

Angry
enraged
furious
incensed
indignant
irate
livid
outraged
resentful

Aversion
animosity
appalled
contempt
disgusted
dislike
hate
horrified
hostile
repulsed

Confused
ambivalent
baffled
bewildered
dazed
hesitant
lost
mystified
perplexed
puzzled
torn

Disconnected
alienated
aloof
apathetic
bored
cold
detached
distant
distracted
indifferent
numb
removed
uninterested
withdrawn

Disquiet
agitated
alarmed
discombobu-
lated
disconcerted
disturbed
perturbed
rattled
restless
shocked
startled
surprised
troubled
turbulent
turmoil
uncomfortable
uneasy
unnerved
unsettled
upset

Embarrassed
ashamed
chagrined
flustered
guilty
mortified
self-conscious

Fatigue
beat
burnt out
depleted
exhausted
lethargic
listless
sleepy
tired
weary
worn out

Pain
agony
anguished
bereaved
devastated
grief
heartbroken
hurt
lonely
miserable
regretful
remorseful

Sad
depressed
dejected
despair
despondent
disappointed
discouraged
disheartened
forlorn
gloomy
heavy hearted
hopeless
melancholy
unhappy
wretched

Tense
anxious
cranky
distressed
distraught
edgy
fidgety
frazzled
irritable
jittery
nervous
overwhelmed
restless
stressed out

Vulnerable
fragile
guarded
helpless
insecure
leery
reserved
sensitive
shaky

Yearning
envious
jealous
longing
nostalgic
pining
wistful

Needs

Many of us have difficulty identifying not only our feelings but also our needs. The following list provides a starting point for identifying your needs so that you are better able to understand them, both for your own personal development and for greater communication and connection in your relationships.

Connection
acceptance
affection
appreciation
belonging
cooperation
communication
closeness
community
companionship
compassion
consideration
consistency
empathy
inclusion
intimacy
love
mutuality
nurturing
respect/self-respect
safety
security
stability
support
to know and be
  known
to see and be seen
to understand and
  be understood
trust
warmth

Physical Well-Being
air
food
movement/exercise
rest/sleep
sexual expression
safety
shelter
touch
water

Honesty
authenticity
integrity
presence

Play
joy
humor

Peace
beauty
communion
ease
equality
harmony
inspiration
order

Autonomy
choice
freedom
independence
space
spontaneity

Meaning
awareness
celebration of life
challenge
clarity
competence
consciousness
contribution
creativity
discovery
efficacy
effectiveness
growth
hope
learning
mourning
participation
purpose
self-expression
stimulation
to matter
understanding

First, all relationships are with yourself – and sometimes they involve other people. Second, the most important relationship in your life – the one you have, like it or not, until the day you die – is with yourself.

Peter McWilliams

THE **i** PYRAMID

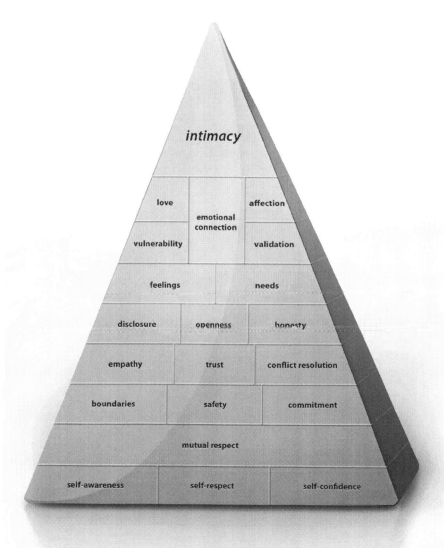

*The building blocks of **intimacy** and **personal connection**.*

Made in the USA
Lexington, KY
30 December 2013